M000045114

HEAD OVER

WHEELS

A 'LUCKY STIFF' TURNS TRAGEDY INTO A CYCLING TRIUMPH

KEN MERCURIO

SUNBURY
P R E S S

Mechanicsburg, Pennsylvania   USA

Published by Sunbury Press, Inc.
50 West Main Street, Suite A
Mechanicsburg, Pennsylvania 17055

www.sunburypress.com

For information about special discounts for bulk purchases, please contact Sunbury Press Orders Dept. at (855) 338-8359 or orders@sunburypress.com.

To request one of our authors for speaking engagements or book signings, please contact Sunbury Press Publicity Dept. at publicity@sunburypress.com.

ISBN: 978-1-62006-498-6 (Trade Paperback)
ISBN: 978-1-62006-499-3 (Mobipocket)
ISBN: 978-1-62006-500-6 (ePub)

FIRST SUNBURY PRESS EDITION: October 2014

Product of the United States of America
0 1 1 2 3 5 8 13 21 34 55

Set in Bookman Old Style
Designed by Lawrence Knorr
Cover by Amber Rendon
Front Cover photo by Jake Morton
Back Cover photo by Kasper Bijlsma
Edited by Allyson Gard

Continue the Enlightenment!

"The Blue Ridge Parkway bike tour would symbolize the ultimate expression of my recovery. It would validate all the support and love I've received over the duration of this unfortunate event in my life, and prove to myself that I could overcome a life-threatening accident and render it just a memory."

Acknowledgments

The author wants to thank everyone involved in my recovery, those mentioned in this book and those not due to brevity, for your invaluable help. I never could have gone through this difficult time without your love and support. Regarding this book, I thank Julie Davey, whom I still hope to meet in person one day, for encouraging me and guiding me in seeking publication after she so kindly agreed to read my first draft. I credit Annette and Julie for the book title—thank you.

Table of Contents

Prologue

"If you do the Simi Ride, you'll get dropped within the first five minutes." A bike-racing friend where I worked at Nestlé said this to me in 2004, but how could I have known his prediction would come true *literally*?[1]

His prediction scared me off from even trying the Simi Ride for three years. It's an informal training ride for professional racers and wannabes like me, and it's been happening since the mid-1980s. It's "advertised" on the Southern California bike racing websites – about how it occurs every Saturday morning between October and February, and how legends Greg LeMond (3-time Tour de France winner[2]) and Andy Hampsten (only American winner of the Giro de Italia) used to do it regularly, and how local Olympian Thurlow Rogers is still its unofficial leader. It was even featured in a *Bicycling* magazine[3] article in 2007! Although it begins in Simi Valley, hence the name, it goes on for 60 to 75 miles to the west through Moorpark, then south into Thousand Oaks, and finally east into the San Fernando Valley.

I've lived in Simi Valley since the early 1980s, but I was not aware of the ride until 2004 when I became more serious about my cycling. But friends knew of the ride and how fast it was. Even my coach I used in early 2007 to prepare me for the Ride Across America had originally

---

1 "Getting dropped" (or "they're going to drop you") is a racing term meaning that you go too slowly to stay up with the pack, and you usually can never catch up again. Although it's worded as if the riders in the pack do something special to make you fall behind, that's usually not the case. You do it all on your own by not being fast enough to stay with them.

2 Since Lance Armstrong and Floyd Landis had their victories taken away due to doping, LeMond is actually the *only* American winner of the Tour de France.

3 Published by Rodale, Inc., Emmaus, PA.

1

encouraged me to do the Simi Ride but changed his mind after he checked it out on the Internet and saw that pros rated it the hardest training ride in Southern California.

But there I was, on November 24, 2007, at 8:30 am, grouped with about 100 other riders, ready to start the Simi Ride. What made me finally think I could stay with these pros? The answer is: Some friends from the San Fernando Valley Bike Club told me I could! Nothing like a challenge from your biking buddies!

I didn't get very far that morning – maybe five miles. On the other hand, I think I traveled beyond where I could have ever imagined, straight into the hands of God.

Chapter One – "Elite"

I joined the San Fernando Valley Bike Club in June 2007, just after the ride across the country, which, of course, had me in the best biking shape of my life. Almost all the riding and training I had done over the previous 15 years had been by myself. Also, except for the riding through Simi to leave and return home, all my riding was done dozens and dozens of miles away – to the north, south, and west, in the countryside and hills.

I had never been in a bike club, other than my company's Carnation Bike Club in the early 80s. While riding through Simi Valley on a Monday morning that June, at the start of a long solo ride, I came across a group heading my way. They said it was a club ride, and that they did Monday and Wednesday rides every week. They also said they were the slow group, and that a separate group of faster riders ahead was where I would fit right in.

The very next day I sent in my membership form and fee and noted from their website the starting place for Wednesday's ride. I drove there the following morning and took off with about 25 riders. It didn't take long for others to welcome me and ask who I was, which attracted me right away. I held my own on that ride, which was about 45 miles for the route I chose. It turns out you can take different routes; everyone rides together for the first 20 miles, ending at a coffee shop in Thousand Oaks where the group stays for 30-45 minutes and socializes over coffee, brownies, smoothies, or other goodies. From there, different people go on different routes depending on ability or length of time you have on a Wednesday morning/afternoon.

In the weeks following those first club rides, I did both the Monday and Wednesday rides with them, and I eventually learned my place in the group, as far as ability. I also was enjoying the socializing and getting to know the others. One thing I learned was that, even at age 56, I was one of the better riders, especially on the hills. The longest route on the Wednesday ride goes over Malibu Canyon Road to Pacific Coast Hwy, southeast to Topanga Canyon, and back into San Fernando Valley over the mountain. I usually would be near the front of the group up the hills, riding my Scattante[4].

It wasn't too many weeks, however, before I headed off on the annual Mercurio family houseboat trip at Trinity Lake in Northern California, on August 10. Little did I know then that this would be the beginning of a terrible two months in my life and the lives of all of us Mercurios. My father had a heart attack on August 15, and I remained in Redding with him while he was in the hospital until September 4, at which time he was flown back to his home town of Hawthorne, 550 miles to the south. He was in a nursing home there for three days, then in a hospital in Inglewood for a week, and finally at home for three days before he died on September 17. I stayed in Redding and then my parents' home in Hawthorne, away from my own home the entire time except one night, for a total of 5½ weeks (more on all of this in Chapter 12).

The one night I did stay at home, about an hour from Hawthorne, was Saturday night, September 15. It was the night before a Malibu Triathlon event, which I continued to aim for even though I was away all that time and was never sure whether I could compete or not. But brother Rick's entire family and sister Cheryl came to Hawthorne to take care of Dad, and insisted I go compete. I had had this event on my calendar since the previous year, when my Nestlé relay team[5], designated the "A Team," had gotten a 5th-

---

4   An all-carbon "store brand" racing bike purchased three years earlier from Supergo, which by then had been acquired by Performance Bicycle.

5   Even though I was retired from Nestlé USA (which had acquired Carnation Company in 1985), I still competed with their 60-member triathlon team. Although one could compete in the triathlon alone, I was

place medal and we were hoping to improve on it for 2007. Therefore, to prepare me for this 18-mile time-trial race, I had taken my bike along on the houseboat trip. I would cycle using my trainer, which is a piece of equipment to which you attach the rear axle of the bike, and pedal against the resistance of a flywheel.

Therefore, even though I was away from home for five weeks, I had my bike and a trainer with me the whole time, and I squeezed in some training both in Redding and Hawthorne. An ominous side-bar story is that on a ride in Hawthorne, about a week before the Malibu Triathlon, I had not gone far when I suddenly crashed to the pavement! I was riding using my aero bars, which cyclists use in time trials to improve aerodynamics and therefore speed. The downside of riding on aero bars is that because your hands and arms are straight forward from the center of the handlebars, you sacrifice steering control of the bike (which is why you never use the aero bars if you will need to maneuver around turns, in a pack with other riders, or on bad pavement). I was on a quiet, newly paved smooth street, but didn't notice a hole in my path, and down I went in an instant. Shame on me!

I suffered about 10 scrapes and cuts on my left knee, side, and hands, and was bleeding pretty badly, but nothing was too serious. Luckily it wasn't worse because I would have dreaded having to go get treated at the nearest emergency room, which would have been the very hospital where I had just spent a trying 10 hours in the emergency room with my dad the previous night and that same morning. I limped the mile home to my parents' house, and cleaned and dressed my wounds as best I could before heading back to Dad at the hospital. So much for that day's training.

Given that I had continued to do some riding and was still in decent conditioning, I went ahead and did the triathlon relay event on September 16. I dedicated the race to my dad, and therefore, maybe not so surprisingly, my time was 1:38 faster than it had been in 2006, and our team moved up to a 4th-place medal. Later that day, I returned to Hawthorne, and during a brief moment of

---

the cycling leg on one of the relay teams.

alertness for my dad, I was able to show him the medal. If you knew my dad, you'd know how much he valued his kids winning awards and medals, since he posted every one in his trophy room. He couldn't really acknowledge what I was showing him, but I'm sure he comprehended and had congratulatory thoughts. It was an emotional moment and I had a hard time not crying out loud. My father died the next day.

When my life got somewhat back to normal schedule, I rejoined the club rides on Mondays and Wednesdays in mid October. My condition was not as good for longer, hilly rides since I had been focused on an 18-mile time trial race, and hadn't been consistently riding at all for over two months. Nevertheless, on a Wednesday ride, I rode at the front of a small group of fast riders on a very hilly route in the Santa Monica Mountains. When the ride ended, a fellow I hadn't ridden with before got to talking with me and mentioned the Simi Ride. I told him I'd heard it was too fast for me, and he said, "Yes, it's fast, but an elite rider like you would have no problem." *The seed was planted.* And, for the first time, someone referred to me as an "elite rider." Wow!

On a later Wednesday club ride in early November, I chatted with both the club president who was probably the best rider in the club, and another top rider. Both had done the Simi Ride so far that year and said I should do it, that I certainly had the ability to stay with them as long as on that particular day I would ride well.

Adding to my confidence was the fact that I had "survived" many of the speedy Rose Bowl Rides over the previous three years. They also are informal training rides for racers, held every Tuesday and Thursday afternoons on the three-mile circuit around the golf course and stadium in Pasadena. You do 10 laps. I truly felt like I'd just won a race when I could stay with that group the entire distance. With average speeds of about 27 mph, it was so fast that some club friends felt I surely could do the Simi Ride.

At about that time, in what would turn out to be a significant symbol and motivator for me in the months to come, I registered to ride in a Blue Ridge Parkway tour in Virginia and North Carolina for the following September,

2008. I originally tried to register for the September 2007 ride, but they were sold out. I first heard about this ride from a *Bicycling* magazine article in May 2007 with a cover teaser saying something like "The Best Bike Ride in America." It was a scenic ride, of course, but it was particularly challenging because in five days and 500 miles, it had over 45,000 feet of climbing. My kind of challenge! Little did I know then just exactly how momentous this ride would become in my life.

By early November, I felt I should give the Simi Ride a try. However, the question was *when*, since they were on Saturdays and I normally felt I had "domestic responsibilities" on weekend mornings. It finally looked like an appropriate time would be the Saturday of the four-day Thanksgiving weekend, November 24, exactly six months to the day after I completed my ride across the country. Interestingly, the following day I would be leaving for three days. I was planning to drive to Hawthorne to rent a moving truck, where sister Janet and I would load it with the things that she and sister Cheryl were saving from the dismantling of my parents' home[6]. Janet and I would then drive it the 400 miles up to her house in Winters on Monday, on to Cheryl's in Santa Cruz on Tuesday, and I'd fly home late Tuesday. Janet had been alone at the vacant Hawthorne house since Thanksgiving night sorting things and preparing the items we'd be moving. She had flown to Burbank on Thanksgiving morning and had dinner with us, after which I drove her to Hawthorne.

---

6   Due to my mom's advanced dementia, we had moved her to a nursing home near Janet's Winters, CA home in late September. More on this in Chapter 12.

Chapter 2 – A fork in the road

I was nervous about the Simi Ride on that Saturday morning, November 24, given its reputation. Also, there was quite a strong Santa Ana wind condition. However, it would be the same for everyone, so it didn't concern me that much.

I left home at about 8:05, figuring I needed to get to the starting point, five miles away in the far eastern end of Simi Valley, well before the 8:30 start. Sure enough, there already were riders gathered at the start. Most had already ridden there from the San Fernando Valley, over the Santa Susana Pass. I saw my club buddies, and the great Thurlow Rogers was waiting at the front.

At about 8:35 the group began riding. The Santa Ana wind provided a tailwind which would push us along during the first 20 miles as we headed west and south through Simi Valley, Moorpark, and Newbury Park. So, even though the pack was warming up through Simi, with its stop lights keeping us from really getting going, our speed was pretty fast. However, it was not at all difficult for me to stay with the pack at that point; the hard part would be coming much later, in the hills to the south.

As we rode down Los Angeles Avenue, the primary artery through town, I found myself in the back quarter of the peloton[7], in the bike lane. There were so many riders that we extended out into the right traffic lane, but I tried to stay to the far right. While stopped at a red light at Sycamore Drive[8] at about mile 4, another rider asked me if I had any allen wrenches in my saddle pack, since his

---

7   The French word for the pack of riders, and it's the standard term all bicyclists use even if we're not French.

8   The street where the city's hospital is located, just a mile north of that traffic signal.

handlebars were loose. I answered sorry, no. I found out later that person was Brady Schroeder. After getting started again, I noticed that our speed had increased. It was still easy to maintain, but I could tell we were going pretty fast so I glanced down at my speedometer and saw 28.5 mph.

The next thing I remember was being in the hospital Emergency Room.

What happened to me was told to me a few weeks later by five wonderful bicyclists who stopped to help me. I'll be forever grateful to Brady Schroeder, Stan Motzkin, Jim Thompson, John Salib, and Lisa Campbell. Brady and John were behind me, and actually saw the crash. The other three were in front of me, but heard the crash and stopped and turned around and went back to assist.[9]

As we were speeding past a park to our south, apparently the right side of my fork[10] just suddenly snapped apart. In a split second, I hit the ground head first, but Brady and John pieced together what they thought happened as follows: After breaking, the right fork segment fell inward into the spinning front wheel. That stopped the front wheel dead (after breaking half of the spokes), which flipped up the rear of the bike and shot me head first into the ground. The forces at work caused the other side of the fork to break as well, and the entire front wheel, with about 12 inches of fork still attached, went shooting across the road to the left. The rest of the bike and I skidded along until we stopped. I had crashed onto my head and then slid on my left side.

When Brady and John first got to me, I wasn't breathing. John yelled out whether anyone knew CPR. Brady remarked that maybe they shouldn't try to move me since I might have a spinal injury. Just about then, they

---

9 A racer friend explained later that the reason no one else stopped was because bike racers are so used to crashes, they are "trained" to keep riding. This was a fast training ride for racers, much like a race, and it is common to just keep going on the assumption that the rider is not hurt badly.

10 The fork is the front of the frame that attaches to either side of the front wheel axle

noticed I had begun to breathe. Jim got there about that time and immediately called 911.

They said I regained consciousness and was asking about sitting up or removing my helmet, to which they told me not to move. Apparently I did complain about a sore neck. I don't recall if they told me what else transpired during the 8 or 9 minutes before the ambulance arrived, but they said they were impressed how quickly it got there. A park service employee drove his truck across the boulevard and placed orange cones around the site so that cars would use only the left lane to pass the scene. The paramedics went right to work assessing my injuries and stabilizing me. They asked me questions, and I answered correctly, indicating that my brain was okay. They asked me to move my feet and other parts of my body, and I did that okay too, indicating that I was not paralyzed. Apparently, one of the bikers even showed me the broken fork, and we marveled at how this could happen.

While waiting for the ambulance, Brady found my cell phone a little ways from the bike, and started to look to see if he could find a number to call to notify someone about the accident. On scrolling through my contacts, he came to "Dad." Brady called "Dad," and only because Janet happened to be in Hawthorne sorting through things at my parents' home, was anyone at that number any longer. He told Janet that her son had had a "serious" bike accident, since he assumed this must be my mother. Janet at first thought perhaps her son Cody had been in the bike accident, but he was supposedly up in the mountains with his father. So she asked the caller where the accident was, and when he said "Los Angeles Ave in Simi Valley," she knew it was I.

Janet asked "how serious?" and Brady responded, "Well, he's breathing." Not much reassurance, but what did they know at that point? Janet asked if he would stay on the phone to give her updates, but soon a paramedic came on the phone and was matter-of-fact in asking her about me – my name, age, if I had any heart or other health problems. Then a policeman came on and asked the same questions, including my address. Janet asked where they were taking me, and he said Simi Valley Hospital and hung up.

In what later would prove to be important, my five companions who helped save my life all looked carefully up and down the street and in the bushes to see if they could find anything such as a stick or piece of metal that could have gotten into my wheel and caused the fork to break. They could not. Once the ambulance left and their search was done, they went on an abridged ride together. It was a few weeks later when I got all their names and phone numbers and could call and thank them and hear their stories of what happened. I felt I owed them my life, but each of them downplayed their role as being the natural thing to do for a fellow cyclist.

The park employee volunteered to drive my broken bike back to my house, which he did after getting my address from the policeman[11].

---

11 We didn't know he had delivered the bike, and Janet kept calling different people for days trying to find where it was. It would be five days before Annette found the bike pieces behind our motorhome in the driveway.

Chapter 3 - "Luck" has two sides, or was it luck?

"Who's that calling on a Saturday morning?" thought Annette. It was the last calm moment she would have for about two months as she walked over to answer the phone.

Janet told Annette, my wife, what she knew, that I'd had an accident, and was breathing, and that they were taking me to the Simi Valley Hospital. Annette was of course freaking out but kept telling herself – out loud – to remain calm. She got dressed and immediately drove the one mile to the hospital, where I was already in the ER. Since she didn't yet know the nature of my accident, she was expecting me to look beat up and broken and in traction. Instead, she said later that I looked "surprisingly intact."

She said the nurse was concerned that I was repeatedly asking the same question, which made Annette think there was brain damage. But then she learned that the question was "What happened?" At that point, no one could answer me. Whatever I had heard about the fork back at the accident scene, I'd forgotten. Maybe it was the morphine, but I'm told that victims in trauma don't remember things very well.

The paramedics used 15 men to lift the board I was on to place me on the ER bed. They wanted to make sure my spine did not move at all. They then *carefully* placed a brace around my neck and another around my chest. The doctor told Annette that I was not allowed to move, yet apparently I kept wanting to, even cycling my legs in the air on an invisible bike. Annette later commented how so many people during the day, the ER doctor, the nurses, and Dr. Dichter (my family physician), kept telling her how lucky I was not to have neurological damage.

I don't have any memory of this early part of my stay in Emergency, but apparently I was speaking and answering questions. They took me away for CT scans, and a short time later the ER doctor returned and informed us that I had "several problems." She said my neck was broken at C2 and C4, I had three broken vertebrae in my back, and three fractured ribs. The neurosurgeon, she said, would be coming soon to discuss my options.

One of the first memories I have from the ER is speaking to Dr. Dichter, who was telling me I would have either a halo or surgery. He mentioned how miserable people are who have a halo, so I recall agreeing that surgery sounded best. It didn't occur to me then, but I thought later how efficient it was for the hospital to have contacted my personal physician so quickly on a Saturday morning, and that he was available and came! I was in good hands.

My memories from that day, as well as the next few, are just snippets. I knew I'd been in a serious bike accident, but in no way was I comprehending the magnitude of what it all meant. As I recall, I was just dealing with each little thing as if it were just "another day at the office." I do remember Annette, Rick and Janet there, and asking Rick what some of the football scores were. I specifically remember asking him how the Kansas-Missouri game came out. I remember pointing out that I was still wearing my cycling shorts.[12] I recall the neurosurgeon, Dr.Virella, telling me that it would take a few days before he could do the surgery because he needed to assemble a top-notch team to assist him. I joked that he wanted an "A" team, and that if he did the operation right then he'd have to settle for the "C" team. I remember him laughing about that. I did not comprehend how serious everything actually was for me. I was not emotional at all.

---

12 To get it off me, the hospital staff had to cut through my PowerBar jersey that I had gotten from Nestle's PowerBar division in 2003 for the inaugural Tour of Hope ride with Lance Armstrong. My sister Cheryl always said that that one time I "raced" with Lance Armstrong I beat him, because he rode only the first 10 miles of the 62-mile ride before leaving for interviews with the press. So, according to Cheryl, Lance dropped out of the ride, meaning I beat him. Ha!

Other than those few memories from the ER, the stories about what happened came from others. I guess my most "famous" remark in the ER was asking Dr. Virella, "Can I cycle again?" He said I *might* be able to in 6 months to a year. When I was told about this the next day, I specifically remember thinking, "Okay, 6 months. That's not so bad. That should allow me to still ride in the Blue Ridge Parkway tour next September." It's funny now to think back how easy I figured it would be to recover, get back on the bike, and just continue as if nothing had happened. The severity of my condition hadn't sunk in yet.

After she called Annette, Janet called Rick, who lives in northern San Diego County about three hours south. Rick had just returned from New York City the night before but was on the road within 15 minutes. He went by Hawthorne to pick up Janet, who had no car, and they went straight to the hospital. They had to wait for quite a long time, but after the CT scan testing was completed, Rick and Janet were allowed in to see me. A friend from Simi also waited for about an hour before they let her in. According to Rick, I "looked helpless and a little pathetic." He said I could look at them by moving my eyes without moving my head. At some point, a technician came in to measure me for my thoracic brace.

The good thing was that, I am told, I was conscious, alert, and seemed optimistic. They said I kept my spirits up, not feeling sorry for myself, and even had a sense of humor. Again, I obviously didn't comprehend the seriousness of the situation. They said I was able to speak clearly and make logical conversation the whole time. I kept wondering where my bike was, what it looked like, and what exactly happened in the crash. Rick turned on the TV in my ER room to watch some football and said I was curious about scores as he gave me continual updates on games. He says I knew which games mattered, so they figured I was "with it." This matches with my memory of asking about the Kansas-Missouri game, since they were ranked numbers 1 and 2 in the country. Rick said I smiled on more than one occasion when I heard a favorable football score.

The various medical staff kept repeating their tests all day to make sure I hadn't lost any neurological functioning. Every so often they would ask me to move my toes, feet, and arms. They'd check eye movement, and ask questions to see how I answered.

Annette called my children, Brian and Katie, and put the phone up to my ear so I could talk with them. I don't remember any of this, but Katie said she made me promise I'd get well so that I could still walk her down the aisle for her May wedding, and I said "of course." Interestingly, the wedding was set for May 24, exactly six months from that day. Brian's initial reaction had a funny twist: When Annette first called him, she had to leave a message and apparently it had static such that Brian couldn't hear everything. What he did hear was that I'd hit my head but, to release the information to him gently, Annette had said "He's going to be okay." Brian took that to mean it was no big deal, and even chuckled to himself as he pictured a scene from the comedy movie Spaceballs, when Dark Helmet crashes his head into a wall and humorously makes no sense in his dazed state. When he got the true story later, he was embarrassed that he had been laughing the first time.

Annette also called her brother Paul, a physician, and her sister, Cathy, an operating-room nurse, to tell them about me but also to ask if they had any advice. Both commented on how serious the surgery would be, and that maybe she should consider transferring me to UCLA. They felt that a university medical center would have been better equipped for complicated spinal surgery than a small community hospital. Should I have asked for a change of venue? Dr.Virella reassured us that he had trained at UCLA and the Cleveland Clinic, and was truly, if he did say so himself, an expert at this kind of surgery. No one, he implied, would be better than he would.

My family stayed with me into the evening when they finally moved me from the ER to a room in ICU. By that time they were getting the good news that the surgery would be the very next morning! Apparently, my neck was so unstable that Dr.Virella felt I needed the surgery as soon as possible. He had been able to assemble the "A" team of specialists in a matter of hours for the Sunday-of-Thanksgiving weekend. To have my surgery so soon was extremely rare, and fortunate.

Now, let's review here. Although I was extremely *unlucky* to have my fork break, and I was *unlucky* that I was going 28.5 mph rather than a more pedestrian speed such as 15 mph when it broke, I was extremely *lucky* in many other ways:

Lucky – I was riding with others. In the past five years with approximately 27,000 miles of biking, about 22,000 were riding alone. In this case, companions were there to provide aid and call 911, and keep me from further injuring myself when I tried to move.

Lucky – The road was smooth and flat. So much of my biking is done on hilly roads, and I easily could have been on a screaming, winding descent with a cliff on one side.

Lucky – I was right in my home town. Although I almost always start and end in Simi Valley, most of my riding is dozen and dozens of miles from here. What a hassle it would have been if my family had to drive back and forth to a hospital 40 miles away. Or, what if the accident had occurred during my Ride Across America in the middle of Ohio or New Hampshire?

Lucky – The call from my cell phone to "Dad" did not actually involve my father being the first to learn of this accident. Had he been alive and taken the call, it's difficult to imagine what anguish he would have endured.

Lucky – There was a neurosurgeon specializing in complex spinal operations right here in Simi to assess my injury and perform surgery within 24 hours. Dr. Virella had moved to this area only a year earlier. Prior to that, a patient with my injury would have had to have been transferred to UCLA. It would have been very dangerous to wait and then move me, given that we didn't know the full seriousness of my injury until after the surgery.

Lucky – I am alive. I am not paralyzed. As you will see, the nature of the injury to my cervical vertebra #2 was so bad that Dr.Virella brought up the "M" word – "miracle." One of the first things he said after the surgery was that normally with this kind of fracture, there is instant death or severe paralysis. How my spinal cord could avoid injury with fractures surrounding it at that spot was truly miraculous.

Luck? Miracle? Divine intervention? My dad protecting me from the world beyond? Various friends and relatives have offered up each of these to try to explain my survival. I have, of course, dwelled on this question endlessly since day one. During the first year after my accident, I clung to the theory of luck, based on my spiritual beliefs up to then in my life. However, since then, what has given me most comfort, peace, and hope is believing that my father and Our Father were sitting together on a comfortable couch that morning watching me ride my bike through Simi Valley, ready to lend a hand when the worst occurred.

Chapter 4 – Hangman's break

Rick, Janet, and Annette were back at the hospital early on Sunday as I was getting ready for surgery. Apparently, I had not had a good night; I wanted to turn onto my side but couldn't, and I kept being awakened by the nurses.

I'm told that I let everyone make a fuss over me while we were waiting. Finally, about 9:20 am, exactly 24 hours since the accident, they rolled me down the hallway toward the operating room, with Annette, Rick and Janet following behind. One of the only memories I have of this day happened as they were wheeling me along – I got dizzy and announced that I thought I was going to throw up. Within a few seconds of saying this, I *did* throw up – twice. GROSS. It went all over my face, my chest, and into my neck brace. I remember the nurses saying something about suction, but that's all I remember. I'm told they did their best to clean me up, but they couldn't do a very complete job of it.

As I was about to have the surgery, Rick said I seemed to be in good spirits "considering they were taking you in to cut you open and put metal in your neck." They wished me good luck one final time and said goodbye. Annette recalled and appreciated the kindness of the anesthesiologist and the "neuro nurse" who assured her that they would take good care of me. The "neuro nurse" explained that her role was to monitor my spinal cord throughout the surgery and ensure that it was okay.

They said it was an interminable wait while I was in surgery. Annette made numerous cell phone calls to family and friends giving them updates, and Rick and Janet did the same. They called Cheryl, Katie and Brian, Rick's wife Beth, his daughters Megan and Sarah, Cheryl's son Miles, and Janet's son Cody. It reminds me of how I did the same thing in Redding and Hawthorne when my dad was dying, as the cell phone bill rose to hundreds of dollars but you didn't care.

Finally, in early afternoon, after a longer time than promised, Dr. Virella came out and spoke with them. The 4½-hour operation had gone well, but the damage was even worse than he had thought. I had broken cervical vertebrae #s 2 and 4, thoracic vertebrae #s 4, 6, and 10, and three ribs. That much they knew going in. What they didn't know was how bad the break was on cervical #2, which is the most critical vertebra in the neck. It has a unique shape because it is the pivot point for the neck and head. Dr. Virella said it had snapped laterally all the way through it, and he had "no idea why" it did not injure the spinal cord that runs in between. He used the word "pulverized' to describe the bone. This kind of break had a name, he said: Hangman's Break. He specifically said to my anxious family that he was surprised I had not died instantly or become a quadriplegic.

Hangman's Break got its name, of course, because the cause of death from a person being hanged by a neck noose could snap the cervical #2 bone, which in turn fatally injured the spinal cord. Most Hangman's Breaks occur from falls that hyperextend the neck, which is exactly what happened to me. However, in only a small percentage of cases does this hyperextension not also injure the spinal cord due to a broken piece of the cervical bone coming in critical contact with it. Any injury or slightest cut to the spinal cord results in paralysis, and of course the greater the cord damage, the more extensive the paralysis is, up to and including death.

Dr. Virella mentioned then and many times since, that when he saw how badly my cervical #2 was pulverized, he would have completely expected this amount of trauma to have pushed the bone pieces into my spinal cord. Bone on both sides crushed and fragmented, but nothing touched the cord in between? He felt that was impossible! He always mentioned Christopher Reeve's injury that made him a quadriplegic, and told me that my injury was similar to his. He always said it but didn't have to: "Ken, you were very lucky indeed."

As time has passed, I have guessed at an explanation for why I was not paralyzed: Perhaps my head hit the pavement so directly from the top, perfectly straight downward, that all the force compressed along my spine lengthwise, and not in any kind of lateral direction into the spinal cord. However, even though I may have been in a straight-down position when my head hit, I was still moving forward at about 25 mph. Thus, as my head hit, there should have been a lateral force pushing the crushed vertebrae bones into my spinal cord. That that did not happen, I can say only: Thank you Father.

Dr. Virella had stabilized the first five cervical vertebrae using two rods and nine screws. The two rods were placed at the back of the spine on either side of it, and five screws held in one rod, and four screws the other. The screws went in laterally through the rod and were fastened into the solid parts of the vertebrae bones, one screw for each vertebra except #2. We noted two months later, on seeing the X-rays for the first time, that he used only nine of the ten screws since he could not utilize vertebra #2. That led many people who saw the X-rays to hit on the joke that I must have a "loose screw". We also learned later that he applied a new high tech, expensive ($7340 list price as noted on my bill) bone-stimulating protein gel called BMP to help speed the development of the new fused bone. Yes, my first five vertebrae have become a single new fused bone instead of separate vertebrae.

In an interesting side note, this bone-stimulating protein was soon banned by the FDA for use in neck surgeries! FDA had too many reports of life-threatening side effects. I describe in Chapter 20 the throat problems I developed and sought medical treatment for, never knowing until years later that they were related to this protein applied during surgery. I will explain there more about this biotechnology protein and why the FDA banned it.

After my surgery I was taken back to the ICU bed, and my family was able to visit me. One of the few memories I have during this time is that I repeated the same gross event that happened prior to surgery – I again threw up while they were wheeling me in the gurney. I guess the movement made me sea sick. Anyway, I'm told I was pretty much out of it while in ICU. My optimism had faded, and I seemed a little miserable. I have a vague memory of someone encouraging me to look at the X-rays of my neck with the new hardware, which I remember doing, but I don't remember what they looked like. I also have a memory of commenting on how bad my throat felt, and they said it was because of the ventilator tubes during surgery. I stated that if my throat felt that bad after only 4½ hours of a ventilator, think how horrible it must have been for my dad who had a ventilator for a whole week, whose throat never did recover. I guess I got pretty emotional on this point.

Of course, I was still on morphine, which affected my mood. When the hospital bill came two months later, with its seven pages of line items and every medication I received, I counted up the morphine doses during the first three days; I had 16 of those mind benders! When I was in the Swiss hospital in September 2004, following my hip surgery (yes, another fall from the bike – see page 99), I was also on a lot of morphine and it caused me to be hyper-talkative. I had called seemingly everyone I knew in America and Switzerland from the hospital bed. In just two days in that hospital, I racked up 720 minutes of calls.[13]

Rick had to head home from the Simi Hospital after a couple more hours because he worked the next morning. Janet, as I am, is retired, so she stayed until Tuesday, at which time she borrowed my car to go back to Hawthorne to continue sorting through everything there. It sure was a huge boost for them to have come right away the way they did and provide support to me and to Annette. It foretold the vast amount of grateful love and support I would receive in the coming months.

---

13 Lucky for me that I was using Nestle's calling card, and that they later felt sorry for me and paid for it.

Chapter 5 – Sprinting to beat the traffic lights

I started biking seriously in 1979. Since I attended college at UC Davis, you'd have thought I would have been more of a cyclist then, since Davis is voted as the best cycling city in the country. Then, as now, almost every student and professor rides a bike to campus and to classes. The busy bike-route intersections on campus even have roundabouts to control traffic flow. Like others, I rode a bike when I was at Davis, but it was only a clunker. I rode to classes and to downtown but did no pleasure riding. I was a runner on the track and cross country teams, not a cyclist.

In 1979, I hired Bob Brown into my Nutrition Research group at Carnation Company in Van Nuys. He was an avid touring cyclist, who had led a BikeCentennial ride across the U.S. three years earlier. He had been with his wife in the Peace Corp in Guatemala, and when his term ended, he and another guy rode their bikes from Guatemala to Texas, and then Bob joined his wife to continue the ride north and west to Oregon. He had scores of other epic tour rides he had done and talked about, and eventually I became interested in biking. Coincidentally, he also went to UC Davis for undergrad and UCLA for grad school.

Carnation Research hired others who were actually bike racers, and soon there was a cadre of us who were always talking bicycles. I finally bought my first real road bike in 1980. It wasn't long, however, before I wanted a better bike. More gears, lighter, better components. I think I rode that first bike only six months before I bought my Nishiki International, a 12-speed. With my Nishiki, I became a real cyclist.

Carnation had lockers and showers, so about 15 of us decided to ride to work three or four days a week.

Wednesday was the day we would drive and exchange all the dirty clothes with four days' worth of clean clothes. I lived in Canyon Country, so I had a hilly 20-mile commute. What made me a better rider was that I rode with a racer, Dave Preszler, who also had gone to UC Davis. Dave was so hardcore that when I bought my Nishiki, the first thing he said was that I needed to immediately remove all the "unnecessary" stuff that only added weight, like the kick stand, the reflectors, and I forget what else. My mom gave me a gift, a radio that attached to the handlebars, and when Dave saw that for the first time, he told me he wouldn't be seen with me if I kept that on my bike. I ditched it.

We even created a Carnation Bike Club, which was supported by the company. I think we had about 30 members. We got real wool jerseys with the Carnation logo, and I still have mine. We went on occasional weekend rides as a club, but these didn't last too long because of the differences in ability that gradually developed. Some of us did ride together on weekend rides, but we grouped ourselves with similar-ability riders.

One thing I never forgot, and now that my fork broke, it creeps me out even more, was that Dave Preszler's fork broke once too. Luckily, this was before carbon fiber, and steel doesn't just break completely with no warning. He was riding home to Newhall, and had just descended a very steep hill. When Dave descended a straight hill like that, he held the handlebars in the front-center to increase his aerodynamics, much like using aero bars (which hadn't been invented yet). As with aero bars, you have poor control of the bike when you hold the bars that way. Dave's speed was over 45 mph on that descent. On this occasion, his bike felt wobbly when he got near the bottom, so he got off the bike to check things out, and the fork came apart right in his hands. If that fork had fully broken off while he was descending, he'd likely have died because, as with most bike racers in the early 1980s, he didn't wear a helmet. Just as it was uncool to have a radio on your handlebars, it was unstudly for a racer to use a helmet (back then; now it's required in races). We all knew Dave had barely escaped death. And, that was what it took for

Dave to start wearing a helmet. Until my fork broke, Dave's was the only time I'd ever heard of a fork breaking on its own, in the absence of a crash.

In April of 1982, I moved to Simi Valley. There were three of us Carnation bike-commuters here including Bob Brown. We usually rode the 22 miles into work separately, because we tended to leave home at different times and we didn't want to wait somewhere to gather. However, back then, everyone ended work at exactly the same time (it's almost as if a whistle blew at 4:30, which will be hard for workers nowadays to believe), so we always rode home as a group. Even a few who didn't live in Simi Valley would join this ride because it was fast and fun, and several were true racers. This was where I *really* learned to ride and handle a bike. We went screaming across the San Fernando Valley as if we were racing, because back then the traffic signals were timed, and it was macho if we could race and beat a light. We knew which ones were possible to beat, and we knew for which ones we could slow down and recover, to prepare for the next sprint. Then, those of us going all the way into Simi had the Santa Susana Pass to climb, and we'd see who could be first to the top. Bob Brown almost always was. I never ceased trying to stay up with them, which is how you get to be a better cyclist. Yes, 44 miles a day of this type of riding made me pretty darned good. Ahh, those were the days!

A big event for the Carnation Bike Club was the 1982 Davis Double Century. Even though I'd gone to UC Davis, I hadn't heard of it. Bob Brown and Dave Preszler had. Boy, was this a big deal in my biking memory! I had ridden century events (100 miles), but a 200-mile ride would be far more demanding. I recall worrying about it, wondering if I was riding enough to prepare, how I'd pace myself, whether I'd finish before dark or whether I'd need to carry lights. A whole bunch of us went up there. As it turned out, I finished while it was still light, in 11:20 (not including the lunch break). That time was respectable. Besides, I had three flat tires in the first half, and had only one spare tube. So, I had to use a patch kit to repair the second and third flats, meaning I lost a lot of time. At the one-hour lunch break, I never had much time to rest because I was buying and installing two new tubes.

Between then and mid-1984, I did lots of centuries and two more double centuries. The double for 1983 was the Tour of Two Forests, which started and ended in Palmdale. It was famous for having over 10,000 feet of climbing, giving it its killer reputation. I was so good on the hills that at the halfway lunch stop near the Pine Mountain summit, I was in third place (a single rider and tandem were in front of me). My father followed me most of the day as my personal cheering squad, meeting up with me after about 40 miles and following until the end. We ate lunch together at the Pine Mountain Inn, and then I was off to see if I could maintain my high placing.

I couldn't. I faded after about 150 miles, and rested for 20 minutes in my dad's car. The final 62 miles were agony, against a headwind. The lucky thing is that it was flat. During that stretch, three all-male tandems passed me, and a single rider caught me and we rode together for the final 30 miles. He was a racer from Santa Barbara. I remember looking at my odometer counting down the miles to 200, and when we finally got to 200, we were still 12 miles from Palmdale. It turned out the ride was 212 miles, not 200! That does a nasty trick to the brain. Those extra 12 miles felt like hell. Your brain is telling you that you should be done, eating ice cream and lying on your back. Yet there's still road ahead, and it seemed like those 12 miles were 100 miles. We finally rounded a corner and could see the finish. At that moment, the "friend" I had ridden with and commiserated with for 30 miles dashed off to finish second of the single riders, and I was the third, seventh overall. Luckily my dad could drive me home because I was in no shape to drive. He took me to a restaurant, but all I could eat was ice cream since my throat was raw from the dry wind all day. I felt like a kid who just had his tonsils out.

Years later, a Nestle colleague attempted the Tour of Two Forests (he didn't finish), and said they had posted the top finishing times in the history of the event, and I was in the top 10% or so! He told me he hadn't known I was such a good rider.

My 1984 double century was another Davis Double, but this time I was the only Carnation person there. No flat tires this time, but also, I didn't finish. I did the first 100 miles in a new personal best of 5:15, and still had the second hundred in front of me. I bonked and had to stop at the 175-mile rest stop and get driven back in the SAG bus.[14]

By mid-1984, I had transferred from the Carnation Research Lab in Van Nuys to the Carnation Corporate offices on Wilshire Blvd in Los Angeles. That meant no more riding to work, which meant I didn't train nearly as much as before, which in turn meant I wasn't as good a rider. I did a few more Solvang Centuries, but my cycling tailed off to a large degree. Then my Nishiki was stolen out of my open garage on a weekend, and that helped seal my "change of life" as far as cycling was concerned.

---

14 SAG stands for support and gear, and refers to vehicles that ride along to support the riders. It also is used for rest stops, as in "SAG stop." It is also used as a verb, as in "I had to get sagged to the finish."

Chapter 6 - Don't sneeze

Recovery. It's a word used every day by cyclists and other endurance athletes. It's as important for success as the workout itself. It's necessary to complete the hard ride. It's vital between intervals. Recovery during a long ride as you tuck in behind another rider to draft and get ready for the next effort. Recovery as you ease up in your descent after the long effort uphill. Recovery with an easy spin for one day, or two at my age, following an intense race-type ride. You need to let the body and muscles rejuvenate so you can perform even better the next time. We speak of recovery as it relates to every aspect of our daily bicycling.

This recovery, though, as I lay in the hospital bed, was a different type. A bigger, broader, much longer recovery. Not just torn muscle fibers rejuvenating, but bones, joints, surgical incisions, bruises, cuts, and scrapes needing to recover. And a spirit.

As much as my spirit had impressed my family in the ER and while I was on morphine for a couple days, I soon entered a phase where I needed to dig deep to get through my new dismal reality. The gravity of what I'd done was finally settling in, as I became more uncomfortable physically. I had long hours to lie there and think about what *had* happened, what *almost* happened, and how my life would be changing. I was actually quite miserable during the nights, all alone for so many hours in that ICU room. I'd think about how close I came to death and what that would have meant to my family. We had recently been through unbelievable trauma with my father, my mother needing a new level of care, our family cabin burning down, and then clearing out the home where we grew up and where my parents had collected our lives in trophy cases, file cabinets, photo albums, and storage boxes. Now I was the cause of yet another worry for everyone.

I also had hours to think about my future, as the night hours dragged on when no one was around. Why did this happen to me? Am I always going to be in this pain? Will I be able to ride again? *Should* I ride again? When will I be able to feel and *be* closer to normal again? Why can't I get comfortable? Will I *ever* get comfortable? How can anyone sleep wearing this damn neck brace? Why can't I fall asleep so I don't have to keep thinking about this stuff?

I'm actually proud to say that this "feel sorry for yourself" attitude occurred for only a short time – Tuesday and Wednesday nights, to be precise. Something in my heart allowed me to view almost exclusively the positives about my survival, recovery, and my life in general. I am thankful to our Creator to be blessed with this optimism.

By Friday morning, I emerged from any doldrums of wondering when I would feel better. Dr. Dichter had to give me pep talks on his daily morning visits. He was the first visitor I had each morning, and I complained to him on both Wednesday and Thursday mornings how lousy the previous nights had gone and how I was feeling pretty miserable. It's absolutely true that all the visitors, cards, well wishers and calls helped tremendously, but I think the primary reason I felt better mentally by Friday was because I felt better physically. And I felt better physically because I finally slept through the night. And I finally slept through the night because of several improvements: We got the pain medication routine figured out, I was getting used to having the neck brace on all the time, they removed the damn IV tubes which meant they didn't need to wake me up so often, and I could turn onto my side to get comfortable. So, I felt better physically, and my spirit had recovered.

During my week in the ICU, Annette went home in the evenings and tried to get things done. She had called her niece Pamela, who lives in the San Fernando Valley, to ask if she'd come stay to help out, namely, to take care of the dogs. She did and was helpful for three weeks before going home for the holidays to her family in Nashville.

My memory didn't return fully until Tuesday of that week. On that day, two friends visited and I asked one to sing me a prayer, although they refer to it as chanting. Her singing had always sounded so nice, even though the words are in Farsi so I didn't know what they meant. But with my eyes closed, her voice wound a path through my soul, and I got weepy knowing she was talking to God on my behalf.

The physical things I recall about those first few days were my sore throat, rarely opening my eyes, and not having enough breath to speak louder than a whisper. I would be rudely reminded that I had broken ribs every time I might want to laugh, take a deep breath, or cough. LUCKILY I never once had to sneeze during the first month while those ribs were healing. I don't know about you, but one of the most painful things I had ever felt was when I once had broken ribs and had to sneeze. An excruciating pain burst through my entire body, especially where the broken ribs were. I can only imagine what pain there would have been this time, with all my additional new wounds and fractures. Another good fortune, to not ever sneeze!

I had a persistent fever, and the doctors kept trying to figure out its cause. Was it a throat infection? Should they give me antibiotics? It eventually subsided on about the fifth day. My sore throat was actually one of my major annoyances during my hospital stay. I sipped water a lot and tried to swallow often because my throat was raw, and I would get phlegm that nagged me constantly. I just couldn't seem to swallow it or cough it away, and it hurt. Of course, I couldn't really cough due to the sore ribs, so I was limited to trying to swallow. This kept me from sleeping too. It seemed like I was awake all night for the first four nights. I recall on Wednesday night dozing off repeatedly, and upon waking, looking at the clock to see how long I had just slept; it was never more than two minutes. Can you imagine doing that all night long? It also felt lousy to remain lying on my back constantly, which also made me think about my father doing that for 5 weeks. I kept breaking into sobs whenever I thought about what Dad had gone through.

Speaking of my father, while he was in ICU at two different hospitals, it seemed that the nurses *never* responded when he pushed the call button. I always had to go search out a nurse for him. First I'd stand at the doorway to try to get their attention, and when that didn't work I'd have to go find someone. So, it was a pleasant surprise to find that the nurses in my ICU immediately responded whenever I pushed the button. During the days, Annette was able to help me. As much as the nurses do for you, it's significant how much a personal helper can do to make a patient comfortable. I couldn't reach the buttons to make the bed move up or down, so Annette would do it. She'd find the water, or a food item, when I needed them.

A highlight on Tuesday was when three San Fernando Valley Bike Club members visited. I really enjoyed "talking shop," and finding out how the Simi Ride had actually gone since two of them had ridden in it. We all marveled at how my fork could have broken. The bike club president, Keith, said that he heard about my accident from Stan Motzkin (one of the five who helped me when I fell), who is a club member, and Keith told another club member that I *almost* died. That guy then put out an e-mail to lots of people and neglected to use the word "almost." Keith said he freaked out when he read the other person's e-mail saying I had died, and quickly called him to get him to correct the mistake.

On Thursday two other riders from the bike club visited me. By then I was up to telling even more stories and laughing with them about their stories – and *their* bike injuries. One thing I learned about cyclists was: We like to compare our crash and injury stories.

Chapter 7 – Good day sunshine

Walking! A highlight of each day starting Monday was having Melissa, the physical therapist, come by to take me for a walk (using a walker, of course). Taking walks lifted my spirits! To walk meant to be the master of my environment again. Melissa taught us how to get me in and out of the chest brace, which I needed to put on before I could sit up. I needed to roll myself onto my right side by pulling on the bed rail, and she'd put the brace under my back. Then I needed to roll the other way and pull myself onto my left side so she could pull the Velcro strap out from under me. Then she could fasten the Velcro strap on the right side of the brace, and I was ready to sit up.

"Willing" and "able," however, were two different things, especially on my first few efforts. I had so much pain as I would push and get lifted into a sitting position from my right side. Once I stood up, though, it felt great, and I could move along – slowly – without a problem. Heck, the four legs of the walker kept you from having to do much effort. Lying back down again from the sitting position, however, was equally excruciating. Melissa had taught me that the only proper way to lie down was onto my side, then to roll onto my back. However, on an occasion later in the week when I got up to use the bathroom, the nurse advised me to lie directly onto my back, saying "trust me, I've done this many times." Well, that one REALLY hurt and I cried out in pain. Later when I told Melissa about it, she just sighed and said some nurses just don't know what they're talking about. Speaking of mistakes, the chest brace had arrived on Monday before Melissa came for my first walk, and a nurse had put it on me. Melissa laughed because it was on upside down, despite someone having printed "top" and "bottom" on it to prevent that very mistake.

When Annette sent an e-mail to some of my Ride Across America buddies on Tuesday night informing them of the accident (which one of them forwarded to the entire 28-person tour group), she mentioned that I had walked a full lap of the ICU. I got a few get-well e-mails from them making fun of my doing a lap, wondering if I ventured off to explore nooks and crannies the way I had in the Ride Across America. I had a reputation on that ride for exploring off the beaten path. As I said, I'm glad my fork didn't break on one of those solo excursions in some far-off place.

On Friday morning Dr. Dichter said he thought I should be able to go home the next day, so we had begun to think through this "new paradigm" in my life. Gosh, going home. I *must* be getting better! Wonderful. Fabulous! But what will we do about X, Y, and Z? I'd need a hospital bed, wouldn't I? During Dr. Virella's visit later that day, I asked him whether I'd be needing a hospital-type bed for when I went home. He flatly said Heck No, I wouldn't need that. "But our bed is upstairs," Annette said. No problem, he can walk up stairs! (His tone was, "What are you, a wuss?" I liked it!)

When Melissa came that afternoon, we told her about the stairs and she said we'd go practice them. We walked until we found a set of stairs that weren't being used, and sure enough, we climbed up and down them, although she held on pretty tightly since I was a bit wobbly without the walker under me. I also was free to go walking on my own, which I did a few times. I ran into Melissa on the floor, and she congratulated my progress. I remember telling her that she was my favorite hospital caregiver, probably because she represented my freedom, but also because she had a pleasant personality.

I need to mention my stink. I hadn't had a good bath or shampoo since the previous Friday morning when I still had an intact neck. I didn't shower before the bike ride on Saturday, of course, and I *did* ride for 10 miles before the accident. And then add six more days on top of that. Good lord, I couldn't stand myself. Okay, the nurses did a bed bath a couple of times which definitely helped (especially the first one), but my hair was yucky, and I still smelled bad. Unfortunately, this state of affairs lasted until December 6, fully two weeks after my previous shower. Only then was I able to take a real shower; more on that later...

Dr. Dichter knew I was ready to go home when he saw how feisty I was getting. On his Friday-morning visit, I questioned an iron pill the nurse said had been prescribed. I had asked the nurse how many milligrams were in the pill, and when she said 325 mg, I refused to take it. I felt that much iron was unnecessary, and would likely cause GI problems. Dr. Dichter said it was he who had prescribed it, because I had lost three units of blood during the accident and surgery, and my blood test showed I was anemic. When I questioned the amount, 325 mg, he said it was common to prescribe that much iron three times a day, and he had prescribed it only two times a day, so I should be happy. I emphasized the downside of taking that much iron, and he just said I didn't have to take it if I didn't want to, which I didn't. (I learned later it was only 65 mg of iron, which I would have taken without an argument. They were quoting me the milligrams of the entire chemical compound, not the amount of just the iron portion.)

So, by Saturday we were getting ready to go home. Janet left that morning on the train that stops in Simi Valley. Cathy, Annette's sister, was arriving from Virginia, and Pamela (the niece taking care of our dogs) picked her up from LAX. Cathy is a nurse and was thoughtful enough to take a week of vacation to help us as I was going from having a hospital staff taking care of me to having to figure all this out ourselves at home. Everyone started hustling and bustling with all the necessary discharge paperwork and getting me supplies. They told me I would have the benefit of a home healthcare therapist, but her first visit couldn't be until Tuesday. Thankfully, we had Cathy.

After we got a portable commode, a walker, and certain supplies, and all the paperwork got signed, I could finally leave. They had to discharge me in a wheelchair, and I remember going outside and being in the sun for the first time since my accident. That by itself – being outside on a sunny day – was another huge spirit-lifter for me. I remember singing "Good Day, Sunshine" to myself. And going home! To repeat one of my lucky breaks, I had a trip of only 5 minutes to get home, instead of half a continent had my fork broken while on the ride across the country.

Getting into the front seat of the car was a little awkward. The roof was too low for my head to get under unless I carefully bent my body far to the side to gain the mere extra inch I needed for clearance. With my two braces, I could not bend over, which is the natural movement to get under something. Cathy also had to remove the head rest since we didn't know how to adjust it backward to get it out of my way.

I had a gingerly time getting out of the car at home too, but soon used the walker and went into the house. Annette, Janet and Pamela had rearranged the house for me. They had removed our love seat from the family room, and put our recliner chair in its place – facing the TV. I would be spending 95% of my waking hours in that recliner chair until the braces came off 12 weeks later. They also removed the two throw rugs in the family room so that I wouldn't trip on the edges of them, and set up the downstairs bathroom for me with all my various stuff.

The recliner was perfect for me. The arms were high enough that I could reach down to support my sitting movement, and they were at the right level for pushing myself up to stand. The best part, though, was the reclined position. It allowed my head to rest gently back, plus I could loosen the chest brace which always provided such a relief. They put a small table next to me to place beverages, papers, and other items I might need. I got pretty good at feeling for things there, since I couldn't turn my head to look where something was.

The recliner was perfect for eating too. I consumed 100% of my food and drink in that chair in the reclined position. I had to release the neck brace to be able to chew, and this I could do since my head could rest backward. I would hold the bowl or plate up to my mouth and pretty much shovel the food in. My various caregivers pre-cut my food into bites, and made sure the bowl didn't weigh too much given that I was instructed not to lift anything more than two pounds.

Yes, that was my "recliner life" for the next month, sitting there visiting with people who would set a chair directly in front of me since I couldn't see them otherwise; getting waited on; reading my many cards from well-wishers; watching TV; reading the paper; talking on the phone; and shoveling food into my mouth.

That actually wasn't all I did. I exercised as much as I could. I still hoped to get back on the bike in six months and possibly still ride the Blue Ridge Parkway tour I had already registered for. I walked laps around the house, took walks outside, and generally tried to move as much as possible. I'd been inspired by stories all my life about people who'd made remarkable comebacks from devastating injuries, and I planned to do the same. If Greg LeMond could recover from a near-death shotgun accidental shooting to win his second and third Tours de France, surely I could recover and ride the Blue Ridge Parkway.

Chapter 8 – Angels and grief

I was truly a blessed person, sitting there on my throne. When I got home from the hospital, I was able to read cards that had arrived and see the flowers and plants friends had sent. Friends came to visit, and friends called. Everyone was so thoughtful. Angels were everywhere, and I'm sure I was with spiritual friends as well.

Annette now had to take care of a lot more things; I used to do most of the chores, and now she had to do many of them. Cathy was the unexpected angel. She took command of managing what I needed. In addition to her skills as an operating-room nurse, Cathy has an innate talent for modifying clothes, equipment, room set-ups, etc. to make activities of daily living easier. She also had years of experience caring for her mom, who had advanced Parkinson's.

Since the home healthcare therapist wasn't going to arrive until Tuesday, it was a good thing Cathy was there to help with my walking, bathroom, food, bed set-up, and personal needs. We wouldn't have known how to do so many things had Cathy not been here, such as how to position the walker going up and down the single step in our entryway, how to get shirts on and off, how to set up pillows in the bed at night, making sure I was in the correct position when taking medications, making sure I walked using slip-resistant shoes, helping me to wash myself and get dressed while lying in bed, and setting up food in the refrigerator in small containers so that I could get things myself if needed. Cathy pitched in on chores too, like washing dishes, doing laundry, flushing the contents of my urinal, and preparing meals. She had Annette buy special light-weight sport shirts that she then cut up the front and hemmed so that I had more casual shirts I could use that did not have to go over my head (all I had at first were pajama tops, and dress shirts that I used to wear to work).

By the time the therapist came on Tuesday, we had already figured out everything she told us. Cathy did so much that she was Annette's angel too, which was in contrast to her usual devilish self when it came to her little sister. She normally "tortured" Annette all her life, as two-year-older sisters are wont to do, but this time she was an angel.

Cathy noticed that I was getting bed sores on my back from lying on it so much. Also, I hadn't completely healed yet where my back had gotten scraped in the accident. Therefore, she put ointments and creams on my sores and instructed me to sleep on my sides, not my back, so as to let it heal. Luckily, I was able to get comfortable sleeping on my sides even though I was wearing the neck brace, and I did sleep pretty well, thank you. To help, I was taking Ambien, a sleeping pill.

Starting on the second day at home, December 2, friends started calling to schedule visits. It was fun and uplifting for me! We decided to allow two visits on that Sunday (which forced us to tell some well-wishers they'd have to wait). Two months earlier, Rich and Denise Hess, best friends since high school, had invited us to a dinner at their home on December 1. Four other Hawthorne High School couples/friends would be there, two of whom were Bruce and Doris Perry and Jim and Nancy Jackson. Now, the day after their dinner party, Rich, Denise, Bruce and Doris wanted to come see us. We had a good visit. They brought me a card they had all signed the night before. Rich and Bruce talked about their own injuries too, since Bruce had had a seriously broken back from a motorcycle accident a few years before, and Rich was suffering from a bad shoulder. They both thought I was taking too few, and impotent, pain meds. (For the record, I was taking 5 grams of Vicodin every 6 hours or so.)

One significant part of the visit was when we examined the broken bike forks for the first time. I remember being truly amazed to see my front wheel with those sheared, ugly carbon pieces that had been my fork. No matter who visited over the coming weeks, we always brought in this visual aid to impress and astonish.

The ominous part of their visit I did not learn about for another week. They were withholding information from me because they didn't think I was ready to hear such terrible news as they were harboring. It's hard to believe they seemed as jolly as they had, knowing the secret they held. During the middle of the dinner party the night before the visit with me, Jim and Nancy Jackson had gotten a call from the police saying that their son had been in an accident and was in an emergency room. They immediately left for the hospital, and the remaining guests learned later in the evening that the boy had been killed. It's difficult for me to write this. I feel now as I did when I first heard about this tragedy; everyone was celebrating my blessed fortune and recovery, yet here was a death. No miracles. No luck. He had his whole life ahead; I already had a wonderful life. Jim and Nancy had signed my get well card, yet their son was suffering an ultimate ending. So much worse than what happened to me. My cousin Robert's death (1981, age 32) came to mind, in that my uncles then were asking why couldn't these things happen to the old guys like them instead of the young ones?

It was brave and considerate for my four friends to keep quiet about what was tearing them up inside. I later agreed with them that I probably would not have done well hearing it right then. It was bad enough hearing it a week later, but on my second day home from the hospital, I was too frazzled with everything going on to have been able to deal with this heartbreak. When I did call Jim to commiserate after hearing the news, I cried and cried.

After the high school buddies left, local friends John Bruton and Mike Marchesano, a bike racer, visited. FINALLY, it was Mike who was able to tell us all exactly what had happened when I had my accident! He had spoken to Brady Schroeder, who is a friend of his, and gotten the whole eye-witness account. We were all so astonished to hear the details, but at least it settled what had been nagging at me from the first. They were also highly impressed with seeing that broken fork, and Mike said he'd never heard of anything like that ever happening.

Since all bike racers crash, Mike also entertained us with multiple stories of his own accidents. It was hard to believe he walked away from so many, or finished the particular race before realizing how bad his injury was. A funny anecdote he told from the Simi Ride the day before (December 1) was that while they were riding down Los Angeles Avenue during the first few miles, Brady was explaining to Thurlow Rogers what had happened to me the Saturday before. As they stopped for a light just past where I had fallen, Brady lost his balance and leaned into Thurlow, who fell. Nothing serious, luckily, but it seemed like I, Ken Mercurio, made the great Thurlow Rogers fall. Yikes!

I got awfully tired on that first day of visitors and went up to bed early. Cathy insisted that from then on, I should schedule naps in the middle of the day, and she was right. Those naps continued for many months and were critical to my recovery. The only days I didn't take a nap were those when I didn't do very much physically.

The physical therapist had encouraged me to walk often to aid healing, so I frequently did "laps" around the house. Originally, someone walked along with me to make sure I would be okay, but soon I was on my own since I demonstrated stable technique. I got "famous" for doing these laps, and for getting faster. Occasionally I walked outside too, which is where I ran into neighbors and told them what had happened to me. After several days, the therapist told me I could graduate from the walker to using a cane, which made me feel like I was making progress, which in turn was a big motivator. After not too many days using a cane, I was able to get rid of that too.

My most cherished memory from those first few days at home – and in the weeks ahead – was the outpouring of care and love from so many friends and relatives. By then, the word about my accident had been forwarded to just about everyone who knew me. I was overwhelmed with how many phone calls, visitors, cards, and e-mails I received. So many friends brought food and meals for us, and they really did help. One friend had brought about 20 containers with a variety of homemade meals while I was still in the hospital, and we continued to eat those for many days.

I didn't realize how many friends I had. I heard from almost everyone who had done the Ride Across America, my Nestle friends, my Carnation Research Lab friends, my Charlottesville friends, City of Hope friends, the bike club friends, Washington, D.C. work-related friends, Simi friends, high school friends (someone put my notice on the Hawthorne High School website), and extended family. Let me tell you, all this outreach truly made me feel wonderful, which was critically therapeutic to my soul. Having a close, loving, supportive family has always allowed me to feel special, but here it was in spades. I wish every last person in the world could be as fortunate as I have been and am. In a sense, we are all fortunate to have Someone who is always with us for support and love, although this divine source is often accessed only in times of difficulty or tragedy.

Chapter 9 – Pre-Lance

Once my Carnation job relocated to downtown Los Angeles in 1984, my bike riding slowed figuratively and literally. I still rode a fair amount, but it wasn't the same. I was limited to weekends. When the Nishiki bike was stolen I got my new one, a Panasonic. I had never heard of a Panasonic bike, only their household electronics. A friend joked that maybe it was wired for sound. It too was a 12-speed, and overall was similar to the Nishiki.

I actually don't recall just how much or what sort of riding I did from 1984 to 1992. Not working at the Research Lab with all my cycling friends also meant that I was not as close to the sport of cycling anymore either. For example, Greg LeMond became the first American to win the Tour de France in 1986 (and he won again in 1989 and 1990), yet without being among other cyclists during those years, I didn't get as worked up over it as I did later when Lance Armstrong started winning.

There was a spell there when I returned to marathon running and didn't ride much at all. I ran in the 1987 Los Angeles Marathon, but dropped out at the 21-mile mark where my family had gone to cheer me on. I stopped to say hello and could not persuade my legs to get started again. I tried the L.A. Marathon again in 1988, running with a Carnation team. This time I finished, in the respectable time of 3:27. I then promptly retired from marathon running.

We bought a tandem in 1992, which got my interest back up for bike riding, and I found myself taking adventure rides on my regular bike when we weren't doing tandem rides. But my riding was sporadic. What changed all that, and returned me to the biking enthusiast I am today, was what I call the "Lance Armstrong Phenomenon."

As with millions of other cyclists, Lance Armstrong's Tour de France victory in 1999, aired live on TV, inspired me to new goals, adventures, and excitement on a bicycle.

Chapter 10 - Who's president?

The house was abuzz once I returned home from the hospital. Pamela, who was staying in Katie's room, did the grocery shopping. She also took care of the dogs. Cathy and Annette were having to shop for special things for me, like Ensure nutritional supplement, pajamas (my only pair starting out was about 10 yrs old and the elastic was shot), sweat pants, straws (I needed them to drink), handi-wipes, ointments for my back, prescriptions, a new shower fixture with a flexible hose, and special pillows. Everyone was doing favors for me, getting me stuff, and handing me the phone when it rang. Cathy also tackled two reorganization projects since she found a couple of enclaves difficult to navigate: the kitchen pantry and the linen closets. Cathy also kept a keen eye on me and anticipated things I needed and was always jumping up to solve my next want or requirement. She'd hear a noise from our bedroom in the middle of the night and come in to assist with whatever it was. After a time, she also helped me get back my independence by telling me to "Do it yourself." We eventually got to laughing about her "DIY" nagging. Cathy really was an angel.

I often woke up in the night to produce my "waterfalls." The hospital had sent me home with a plastic urinal, and I used it several times each night lying there in the bed. Unfortunately, I couldn't figure out how to make it a quieter process, so Annette had to endure the "grossity" of what was happening right next to her, and this went on for three months until the braces came off.

Speaking of the bed, getting in and out of it at the beginning and end of each day was a major ordeal, and I needed help every time. Annette had organized my new "wardrobe," and would help me put on my pants and shirt while I was still lying down. I rolled from one side to the other as my helper (later including the caretakers) would put on one shirt sleeve at a time, or put the ointments on my back. Then we had to put on my socks and shoes, which wasn't easy. And all this had to be reversed at night, changing into pajamas.

A real shower! This was definitely a highlight near the end of my first week at home! It came on Friday, after I got approval by phone from Dr. Virella that a helper was allowed to support my head while the neck brace was off. Cathy studied the shower and how my portable commode might fit so I could sit down, and thought through the sequence of events that would have to occur for a successful and safe shower. Finally she had it figured out, and explained it to us. With Cathy out for the moment, I stripped down to where I had on only the two braces. I slowly squeezed in and sat down on the commode, facing the back shower wall. I removed my chest brace. Cathy returned, and Annette, wearing a bathing suit since she knew she'd get wet, climbed in and stood at the back corner of the shower. We then removed the neck brace and Annette supported my head with her hands under each side of my jaw, to make sure nothing moved. It felt a little strange taking off that neck brace for the first time in two weeks, but it wasn't like my neck was limp. I think I could have held my head still without help, but better to be safe.

Cathy had remembered to run the water to get it hot before the process began, so it felt good when she finally turned on the water and let it soak me. The shower door was open the whole time, so we had towels on the floor. Cathy stood on the towels right behind me, outside of the shower. Since we hadn't yet installed the flexible shower head, Cathy had to hold a bucket up to the nozzle, let water partially fill it, and then she'd dump it over my head. Oh that felt nice! The first and best part of the shower was the shampoo. I'd had no shampoo for two weeks, and my hair was greasy and yucky, and my head was itchy. Getting clean hair was so great! More buckets dumped over my head to rinse, and then the body washing. I did the front, and Cathy did the back. When we were finished, we dried my head very gently, and then put back on the neck brace.

Eventually we got me dried and into clothes and I could go rest on my recliner, ready now for a shave. I had already had one shave in the hospital (done by a male nurse) and a second one in my recliner (done by Cathy and me), so this was something we knew how to do. It was still quite a process though, and again, it was a wonderful feeling to be all clean and shaven. About a week later I got a second neck brace, which made the process simpler and allowed only one helper, not two. This was because I could leave on the neck brace and let it get wet, taking it off only at the end to let the helper wash my neck while I held my head still. Then, we could put back on the second, dry brace.

During that first week at home, I also got started on all the phone calls related to the caregiver insurance. There were so many calls required, with different aspects of the company wanting to interview me to assess my abilities and needs. They had me call an associated company to search for a local caregiver provider, and they too needed to assess my abilities. Then the caregiver they identified, Visiting Angels, interviewed me over the phone. The main company sent out a nurse to interview me for two hours as to my abilities and needs. Visiting Angels then needed to do the same thing. All these calls and visits involved leaving messages, call-backs, reporting to each other what the others had said, calling my two local doctors to have them fill out medical evaluations on me, etc and ETC. If someone truly is impaired, it seems like the system is such that you would never succeed in getting the assistance you need. Only the ones least in need can persist to get the help that is available out there.

Friend Barbara, a nurse, was visiting me the day the main insurance-company nurse came out for the 2-hour interview (Annette was back to work by then). Barbara went into the living room to leave us alone but couldn't help hearing the questions being asked. We got quite a good laugh afterward about the "mental capacity" test done at the end, *after* the nurse had been quizzing me for 90 minutes about all my medical histories and medications and numerous details that required a perfect memory. So *then* she wanted to know if my brain was all there, so she asked things like what state and country we were in, what kind of place we were in (a house), what year it was, who the president was, to remember three words – table, chair, pencil – and *immediately* repeat them, to write a sentence (any sentence), to copy a simple drawing that she showed me, and to follow the direction on a piece of paper she handed me (which said to not speak a word). WEIRD. I kept cracking up at the stupid questions and tasks, but had to hide it since this nurse was a serious type. At least the Visiting Angels lady's interview was normal. With that woman, we just visited about things, mostly biking.

All in all, it was a good thing it was Christmas time and my family and friends had time off from school to take care of me until my caregiver actually started. Her first day was December 28, and it wasn't until the 27th that everything got approved, even though we were making calls and filling out forms as fast as we could. There were so many steps involved. If I had needed a caregiver right away, tough beans; so again, luck was with me since I had family and friends who could come in once Annette went back to work (on Wednesday, December 5, 11 days after the accident), Cathy had to return home (on Sunday, December 9), and Pamela flew home to Nashville (on December 10).

Chapter 11 – "Don't even *think* about doing that bike ride"

In early December, I went to the dentist to make sure I hadn't injured my jaw or teeth in the accident. I did feel some mouth pain on my lower right side when I chewed on hard food. The dentist said it looked fine to her. She also inspected my three chipped teeth, which had been so minor an injury from the accident compared to everything else, that I almost didn't mention it to anyone. She said she'd fix those teeth later, once I was better physically.

Brian came home from Ohio State for the holiday break on December 8. He helped out some over the weekend but then was alone to take care of me on Monday the 10th. He was very attentive and helpful, but I felt like a real heel since I had to ask him for so many things that others had already learned how to do. He didn't complain though, and it was nice having my son taking care of me all by himself. I recall that he was the one who bought my cane, which the therapist said I was ready to graduate to since I seemed so stable with the walker. So, slowly but surely, I was becoming more independent!

The next day, Bruce Perry, the high school friend, drove all the way here, a two-hour drive. He not only helped with me, but drove Brian to the airport bus in Van Nuys. Brian, it turned out, had a week's worth of business meetings at the University of Hawaii. He was "comparing notes" with others on his doctoral research project, which included professors and grad students from Ohio State, UCLA, University of Hawaii, Washington University, and six other universities.

Two friend visits were helpful – Walter brought his guitar and sang a few songs, and Rosemary brought a DVD movie, which began my three-month barrage of movie-watching. It turned out that City of Hope's patient education department gave us a three-month gift subscription to Netflix -- three movies at a time. By the time the three months were over, I'd seen 50 movies. Fifty movies! (And it went on. I continued with Netflix's one-at-a-time program.)

On Friday, December 14, Annette took me to my appointment with Dr. Virella. Both he and Dr. Dichter had wanted to see me two weeks from the time I left the hospital. We decided to see Virella first. I had to wait about an hour, and it was getting mighty uncomfortable with that chest brace, but finally I was called in. Dr. Virella was his usual confident self, reassuring me that he had done a great job and confirming I was indeed lucky to have not suffered a worse fate. He approved my two exercise requests, to walk on our treadmill at home and to ride a recumbent stationary bike if I could find one at a gym.

This was my visit with Dr. Virella when he realized that my talk about riding a bike again involved something as momentous as the Blue Ridge Parkway. He had said I could *maybe* ride a bike again, and that would be fine, but he imagined me riding slowly along a bike path for a few miles. I thought it was studly and cool to have the Blue Ridge Parkway as a goal, so I decided to get more specific with Dr. Virella to see what he'd say. Once I described what the Blue Ridge Parkway was, and the 5 day/500 mile goal, I'll never forget his response: "No matter what you might be able to do if you recover, don't even *think* about doing that bike trip!"

Instead of shutting up and behaving like a good boy, I immediately began to advocate my chances and to question his rebuke. "If I can ride at all, why should I not ride a long distance if I can withstand the pain?" "The chances of an accident on a busy bike path are probably greater than riding on a low-traffic parkway." Whine whine. Sure enough, I softened him, and he could not elaborate on why he should discourage me if I was determined to get back on a bike in the first place. I now felt emboldened to announce my goal to a few select others!

I had to be careful, though, of sounding too ridiculous at this early stage of my recovery. I didn't want to be counting my chickens before they hatched, because I was many months away from knowing if I could recover enough to even ride a bike at all, much less walk or drive a car without pain, or any other normal activity. So, even though the Blue Ridge Parkway was mostly for me to dream about and visualize for the coming months, it made a huge impact on my psyche and inner spirit to have a tangible goal to motivate my recovery. I would suggest that setting real, achievable goals is THE critical component for anyone needing to recover from ANY setback in life. Also, sharing your goals with others helps motivate you to stick with the effort. Do it!

Katie arrived on Sunday the 16th for her Christmas break from the University of Washington. She was one of the first to see my new "hair do," my first-ever buzz cut I'd gotten the day before. Sister-in-law Beth had first suggested this years earlier, saying that bald spots were less conspicuous if the rest of your hair was short. But whenever I looked in the mirror, it still looked like I had normal hair since I couldn't see my bald spot, and I never had the nerve to make such a drastic change in the way I looked. Then when Bruce Perry visited earlier that week, he started talking about his own buzz cut. It got me thinking: If ever there would be a time when I could make a conspicuous change in my appearance, this would be it. And, it would help with my itchy scalp given the infrequency of my showers. To help seal the deal, Katie heard about my possible decision and kept pushing hard for me to finally look cool in the hair department (relatively speaking). So, a buzz cut it was.

The barber, whom I'd been going to for 25 years, made quite the big deal about my injury. Once he'd done as much as he could with the neck brace on, we removed it, and I held my head steady while he cut at the back. It took me a few weeks to get used to seeing my new look in the mirror, but virtually everyone said they liked it. Nice people always say that, though. Except Katie. She's honest, but even she said it looked much better.

On Monday (December 17th) we went to my appointment with Dr. Dichter. Katie went too, and the story of this doctor visit turned out to be Katie. She went to elementary school with Dichter's son, so over the years, my doctor and I have always compared notes about our children's achievements and whereabouts. After Dr. Dichter and I got our medical business out of the way, which didn't take too long since I was doing well, he and Katie launched into a long discussion about what she and his son were up to. I was a mere onlooker. It actually got kind of funny, the extent of their conversation.

I do remember Dr. Dichter emphasizing how my surgery and recovery had been so remarkable because I was in such excellent physical condition. He said most people would have had many complications and a longer recovery. He continued to mention that to me up to 11 months later, so I must have made an impression on him. He always did tell me how slow my heart rate was, how perfect my blood pressure was, and how my cycling kept me in such great shape. It made me feel good to know that all my hard exercise ended up giving me such a critical side-benefit.

A special highlight occurred earlier that day with the bike club. As mentioned previously, they take their Monday rides in Simi Valley, and my buddies had said during their hospital visit that they'd stop in to say hello on one of them soon. Sure enough, they called that morning to say they were having their snack break in Simi and would it be all right to stop in? Yes! A few minutes later, a bunch of expensive bikes were piling up in the front yard, and in came about eight of my comrades. We all went into the patio and talked for about 30 minutes, and this was so exciting for me. Of course, they all wanted to see the broken fork, and of course they were all amazed. They began to talk about whether I'd bring a lawsuit. They talked about their own accidents and injuries, as bicyclists do. I was so energized.

The next day Jim Thompson, one of the cyclists who stopped to assist me when I fell, came by to visit. It was an honor for me to get to meet him and thank him in person. The day after the accident, he had posted an account of the crash on a cycling forum website, and many had commented on forks breaking and the bad luck of it all. It was kind of strange to see my event "memorialized" on the Internet, as if I were in the newspaper for all to see.

Katie became my caregiver for most of the rest of that week. Brian returned from Hawaii mid week and also helped out. They also visited their mom and step dad Bill (only 150 yards away), so usually only one was at our house at a time. Katie and Brian both had their turns helping me shave, which was fun because after I did what I could, they took the razor and finished the job. I could not bend my neck back, so I had a difficult time getting to spots under my chin and jaw. They were diligent as they found a way to get the missed spots without cutting me.

Katie's primary memory of taking care of me, however, was my "terrible smell," as she put it. "Worst ever," she said. Even though by then I could take showers more easily and often, it was still a difficult process for two people, and Katie said there was no way she was going to be the second person on a shower. So, I still went a few days between showers, and the smell got pretty bad. I couldn't take off and put on shirts by myself, so when Katie was the one helping me do this at the beginning or end of a day, she said it was torture to have to smell me. My loving daughter!

Interestingly, I was able to work at the computer for about 30 minutes at a time before my back would hurt and I'd need to return to the recliner. Therefore, I continued e-mail correspondence with everyone and even did my consulting work. Just before the accident, I had agreed to a big project with Frito-Lay, at the behest of Bob Brown, who was the Carnation cycling friend who had gotten me started as a cyclist in 1979. (He left Nestle for Frito-Lay in 1992.) I called Bob to make sure they still wanted to use me given that I couldn't work too many hours at a time. We agreed to give it a try, and sure enough, we had a big conference call in mid December, and I was to write two papers for them before the end of the year. This was yet another area of my life that I was able to resume which allowed me to "get back to normal," so I really liked doing my consulting (and communicating with friends and relatives on the computer).

One of the e-mails I sent was to Paul Wood, the owner of the company operating the Blue Ridge Parkway tour[15]. I described my accident, but also said I was holding out hope of still doing the ride. Realistically, I truly didn't think at that point that I could recover enough for such a tough ride, but by telling Paul I was going to try, it established a motivator for me. I also had to tell Bob Brown I wasn't yet ready to give up on the Blue Ridge Parkway. He had decided to sign up for the ride once he knew that I had, but he hadn't yet paid his deposit. When he heard about my accident, he figured it was off. But I told him I still thought I *might* ride, so he said he'd go ahead and fully register, and get his buddy in Valencia, Bert Stock (see page 94), to do it too in case I couldn't when the time came. Now there'd be three of us friends doing the ride, which made me even more determined to prepare and successfully complete it.

This is when I first started thinking of the Blue Ridge Parkway ride in terms of symbolizing my recovery. The more I thought about the ride in this way, the more importance it took on for me. It came to represent an ultimate achievement to confirm that I had fully recovered. It would validate all the support and love I'd received over the duration of this unfortunate event in my life and would prove to myself that I could overcome a life-threatening accident and render it just a memory.

But in the here-and-now, it was the time of year for Christmas decorations and a Christmas tree. Normally it was my job to climb the ladder in the garage to get down all the boxes of decorations and to help bring home the tree and set it up. We were so fortunate to have a friend like John Bruton who willingly helped with things like this. He not only did those two chores with Annette but also installed the flexible shower hose for me in the downstairs bathroom. She joked that my accident conveniently got me out of doing all the Christmas chores I grumble about every year, including (shudder) *shopping*. Yes, there was at least this one silver lining in what happened to me!

---

15 The company is called Black Bear Adventures Bicycle Tours, http://blackbearadventures.com/

When the weekend before Christmas came, Annette had the huge job of getting ready for the onslaught of Mercurios. Prior to my accident, we had invited the entire Mercurio Family, who normally would spend Christmas at my parents', to spend it at our house. It was tradition for Annette and me to host my parents and six other family members for Christmas Eve dinners. They would return to Hawthorne after the dinners, and then Annette, Brian, Katie and I would go there the next afternoon along with Rick's family for our big Christmas dinners. For this year, with no more home in Hawthorne, we were going to host the whole affair – Christmas Eve, Christmas Eve night, Christmas Day, and Christmas night.

With my accident, should we still attempt to host this huge Mercurio gathering? Even if I had been in perfect shape, it was going to be a daunting ordeal considering all the people (16), all the sleeping arrangements, all the meals, and all the special events and tributes for Mom and Dad. Megan's new husband, Manuel, and Sarah's fiancé, Anthony, were coming too. Should we?

We decided in early December to continue with the original plan. Family closeness had always been a Mercurio hallmark, and it was more important than ever at this juncture. Now, Christmas had arrived, and we'd be under the gun.

Chapter 12 – Family roller coasters

It's an understatement to say that the Mercurio Family had been through a lot since the August houseboat trip. The drawn-out situation with Dad, getting Mom moved out of Hawthorne and into a care home near Winters (where Janet lived in northern California), dealing with the Hawthorne home where we'd grown up and they had lived for 52 years, and then the final stab in the back – the family cabin in the nearby San Bernardino Mountains burning to the ground in late October. And now we were gathering together for the first time, other than Dad's funeral, to celebrate Christmas.

Every single member of the family, except Brian, Annette and Beth (Rick's wife), had been at Trinity Lake, 600 miles north of Simi Valley, when Dad suffered his heart attack (and Annette flew up the next night, and Beth the day after that). We had been at a spot in the middle of the lake when he needed emergency care early on the morning of August 15, a Wednesday. Rick, Katie and I took him on the rented ski boat to the marina, where we called 911 for an ambulance. Dad could barely breathe that whole time. Rick accompanied him in the ambulance, and I followed by car to the nearby hospital. The doctor there finally told us he had had a heart attack and would need to be helicoptered the 40 miles to Redding for better care. We got to visit with Dad, and he seemed so much better after getting a diuretic, as if he could just go back to the houseboat! He was sitting up in bed and talking normally again, giving us details about Mom's various medicines, and carrying on a typical conversation. This gave Rick and me a high degree of optimism, but as we watched him being put into the helicopter and said our temporary goodbyes, it would be the final time he would ever be that "normal."

All 14 of us, including Cheryl's dog, stayed up there – either at the lake or in Redding -- through the initial several days when everything was so new with Dad's condition. The next time any of us saw him, he was in the ICU in Redding with ventilator tubes going down his throat, so he couldn't communicate. We all wanted to be in that ICU room with him, but we still had to deal with the fact that all our things, and most people, were still back on the houseboat 70 minutes to the west. We had only a few cars, so there were logistical gymnastics going on constantly to deal with everyone. Cell phones were a necessity.

Some stayed in Redding during the first day or two, but most were shuttling back and forth to the lake since we still had to get my ski boat -- whose engine had broken down on the first day -- from a different marina, get it back onto the trailer when it had no working engine, turn in the houseboat, and pack everything into my motorhome. While cruising the houseboat across the lake with my disabled boat in tow, I took a cell phone call from Dad's cardiologist at the Redding Hospital, giving me an update and presenting care options. What an unreal scenario! I had been designated as the official decision-maker on his care, so they had to call me no matter where I was. Things were still so unknown with his condition, yet most of us held out optimistic hope that he would come around at any minute. Once we finally got everyone into Redding, we rented motels near to the hospital, and I had to find a place where the motorhome and boat could go. We found a park about 8 miles south, next to the Sacramento River. Janet and Mom found a Kiwanis-sponsored house across the street from the hospital.

It just so happened my birthday was on Friday of that week, two days after Dad entered the hospital. There seemed to be nothing new with Dad that afternoon, so all 15 of us gathered at the motorhome to eat some of the food left over from the houseboat, and to celebrate my birthday, such as it was under those conditions. Over all my years, I had had some interesting birthday locales given that

August is a vacation month, but nothing ever topped that as being a strange birthday. I didn't want to celebrate my birthday so much as celebrate that we were all there together to support each other at that trying time.

That weekend, four of the group went home according to the original houseboat trip schedule, and on Sunday evening, Beth and Annette went home. But that still left 10 of us in Redding, coming and going from the hospital, dealing with meals, taking care of Mom who needed 100% care for her advanced dementia, and non-stop cell phone calls to figure out where everyone was. Dad's ventilator tubes were removed after a week, allowing us to – very gradually – communicate with him again. He seemed to be relatively stable, so eventually everyone headed home except for Janet, Mom, Cheryl and me. Janet even got a ride back to her home in Winters so she could take care of some things, and to get her car. Eventually Cheryl returned home, leaving Janet, Mom and me. Many in the family came back for visits on the weekends. By then, I had moved my motorhome to the Kiwanis House parking lot across the street from the hospital where Janet and Mom stayed, making it a lot easier to help with Mom and be close to the activity. (I had dropped off the boat at my college roommate's home about 7 miles east.)

It was hard emotionally to be away from home watching over Dad's care and helping coordinate taking care of Mom. At times like that, one doesn't really have time to think about the bigger picture; rather, you just do what needs to be done at any given moment. Dad had forever been our family's linchpin, and now he wasn't, and others had to step up.

After he had been in the hospital for three weeks, we flew Dad down to Hawthorne to rehabilitate, following a "renewal" and his ability to go off the critical medications. That followed a particularly devastating time for the family, when he decided on the Friday before Labor Day weekend to let himself go. He didn't want to continue on, figuring he'd never recover. He stopped all treatment, all IVs were removed, he stopped eating, and they considered him to be on "comfort care," waiting to die at any moment. Since it was Labor Day weekend, many family members were there for those wrenching hours. Even Katie flew in to be able to have a final goodbye. We let other family members say their final goodbyes over the phone we put up to his ear. We were all crying so much, and having to tell the telephone tree about this through more tears. Dad just slept most of Saturday and Sunday, and we all thought, as we sat there watching him, that any breath could be his last.

But then he woke up on Monday morning, Labor Day, feeling better! He spoke more normally, he spoke of things as though he would have a future, he carried on short conversations, he made jokes. When Rick and I had him for a moment alone, we asked if he had changed his mind and wanted to live after all. He said Yes!! Our emotional roller coaster was on the upswing once again! It seemed to me that all he needed was some peace and quiet from all the nurses poking and waking him, and relief from all those medications. Once his body had a chance to recover on its own, he felt better.

The hospital found a "rehabilitation" nursing home in Hawthorne that would agree to take Dad (and was covered by his insurance company). Rick flew the 550 miles with him in the medical transport plane to Hawthorne, late in the day on Tuesday, September 4. Janet and Mom headed to Winters, and I went to my friend's house where my boat was, attached it to the motorhome, and finally headed out of Redding. I had gotten pretty chummy with that town, with my occasional bike trips around the area (one was a 63-mile ride when Rick had returned on a Saturday), but was I ever glad to be leaving for home! It was a strange feeling, suddenly being all by myself, to reflect on what had happened in our family in the previous three weeks. What would become of the Mercurio family? We would likely never be the same again. My moments of reflection, however, kept getting interrupted by cell phone calls. Everyone wanted to know what was happening minute by minute. The cell phone has done that to us.

After the one night in Winters, Janet, Mom and I rode in the motorhome, pulling the boat, down to Simi Valley. Again, we were on critical (and non critical) cell phone calls all day, as we needed to connect with Dad's local doctor, discuss care and medications needed at the nursing home where Dad was, discuss issues with the health insurance company, etc. Within 30 minutes of arriving in Simi Valley, Janet used Mom and Dad's car, which had been in my driveway since the day we left on the houseboat trip, and drove to Hawthorne with Mom. I spent about two hours at the Simi house, unloading food from the motorhome, putting the boat away on the side of the house, putting the motorhome away, and packing my car with the things I would need in Hawthorne. Then, off I went. After three weeks of being the primary caregiver for him, I was focused on getting back to his side as soon as possible. I was still in "another world."

Before even leaving Redding, we were getting calls from my aunt, Dad's sister, that his nursing home in Hawthorne was horrible. Based on information she found on the Internet, she said we needed to stay with him 24/7 to help with the care he needed since this place would, according to her, have no qualified caregivers. So, Rick, Janet and I (who, with Mom, were all staying in the Hawthorne home) took 8-hour shifts with him for the two and a half days he was there. It was heartbreaking to see him again miserable because he couldn't get comfortable in the bed, and he still couldn't eat anything. Nothing tasted good to him, and even when he tried to eat or drink, he would go into a coughing fit. After three weeks of virtually no food intake, he was seriously malnourished. His mood had been so high when he left Redding, ready to rehabilitate back to good health, but now he seemed to be slipping back into pain and misery.

Thus, on Thursday night, after only two days in his new "rehabilitation" nursing home, Janet persuaded them to transport him to the hospital. I replaced her at the nursing home since I was the official medical decision-maker for him, and followed his ambulance to the hospital. I waited with him in Emergency from about midnight to 10 am the next morning, when he finally got admitted to a room. Rick was there for a good portion of those hours, but he was suffering a bad cold, so he eventually returned home. The roller coaster ride was back in full force. While we were glad he was out of the nursing home that had poor care for him, we also knew that he was back into primary care and no longer considered in rehabilitation. It was an emotional challenge to realize what the downsides of this move were, yet try to make everything positive for Dad and others in the family. Not being able to communicate easily with Dad made everything more trying too, since we could rarely understand what he was trying to say.

Dad gradually went downhill after that, even with the good care he was getting. He quickly was put on a feeding tube, which raised our hopes that with nutrition, finally, he would improve. He was feeling reasonably good on Sunday, his third day there, so Rick and Janet went home. Janet had lots to catch up on back at her house, including caring for her son Cody. Although she arranged for in-home caretakers for Mom from 9 am to 7 pm, and Annette began staying at the Hawthorne house to help in the evenings after her work, I ultimately had responsibilities for both Mom and Dad. So it was an extremely stressful week for me. Not to mention all the non-stop cell phone calls to everyone who was anxious for updates.

With Dad having a recurrence of an intestinal pathogen he had in Redding (Clostridium difficilis), it made him incontinent, which in turn made him completely miserable. By Thursday, he was adamant about going home, just to get out of the hospital environment. He came to rely on having someone with him to tend to his every wish, and I couldn't even be with him as much as I had been because I needed to help with Mom.

On that Thursday when he wanted to go home so badly, I wasn't even at the hospital until well after noon. The night before, Mom had gotten three bad wounds on her leg when our dogs bumped into her. It was pretty ridiculous that our dogs were even there at all at a time like this, but Annette had insisted that the dogs be with us in Hawthorne. When she got home from work that Thursday evening, the dogs got hyper as they always did when one of us came home from an absence; in their wild excitedness the dogs banged into Mom's leg. She normally would have been wearing leg coverings due to her paper-thin skin (one of many health problems she suffered), but she happened not to have them on when Annette arrived home. The dog bumping easily tore away her skin in three spots. Since she was on the blood thinner Coumadin, she wouldn't stop bleeding, no matter what Annette and the caregiver did. So, Annette called me home from the hospital, and I took Mom to an urgent-care unit. I now had two crises on my hands, and this second one was so unnecessary.

We got out of the urgent-care unit quite late at night, and I just went to bed and never got back to Dad. The next morning, with Annette off to work, I had to take Mom to her doctor for follow-up care on her leg, and that further kept me away from the hospital. They wanted her leg elevated, so I couldn't take her to her daycare center; I had to wait until the caretaker arrived at noon. Trying to squeeze in bike training at every possible moment, I set up the trainer in the living room in front of Mom and pedaled away, engaging her in conversation about how fast I was riding.

Just as I was leaving for the hospital once the caretaker arrived, I got a call from Dad's doctor who said he was agitated and was demanding to go home. I needed to approve right then and there whether they could release him to come home on hospice care. I knew Dad was suffering and that the liquid nutrition we had hoped would cure him had been too late. I got the doctor to make a prediction that normally they don't like to do – at best, even in the hospital with complete care, she indicated that he would likely not live longer than two weeks. With anguish at that admission, I gave approval for him to come home. I then rushed to the hospital, making cell phone calls to Janet and Rick about the terrible reality we now were facing. However, again, there was the optimistic side of things: He was getting to go home, finally, after four weeks in hospitals. Maybe that would lift his spirits and the liquid nutrition would somehow kick in. The roller coaster ride never ended, but I had no time to ponder things. Annette and I would be the only ones there, and we had to prepare for his arrival later that evening, with deliveries of goods and equipment, nurses to teach me how to care for him, and paperwork to sign.

As you know, the coming-home celebration didn't last long. His spirit was lifted only for about the first four or five hours. It was a tough night for Dad and me. We got little sleep, and Dad was just as uncomfortable as he had been in the hospital. Friday was no better, and I was exhausted. Annette got vertigo, so she stayed home and lay most of the day in the back bedroom. At that point, I was taking care of, or responsible for, Dad, Mom, Annette, and the dogs. Thankfully, Rick's entire family came on Friday evening, and I finally got to sleep through the night (Annette felt well enough in the evening to drive home with the dogs).

When I awoke Saturday morning, I learned that Dad, during the night, had decided not to keep trying. He told Rick he wanted to go off all medications and food and water again. He was mainly sleeping, so I decided, with encouragement from Rick, to go ahead and do my triathlon relay race the next day. It was a way to get the terrible reality off my mind for a few hours. Cheryl also was coming for the weekend to help, so I left Saturday morning about 10, went to a Nestle guy's apartment a few miles away to get my team uniform, went to Malibu to check in and get my racing number, and then went home to spend my first night in my own bed in over six weeks.

I headed out to Malibu on Sunday morning at 5 am. As I mentioned in Chapter 1, the race I dedicated to my Dad was pretty fast. In fact, my average speed of 22.2 mph was a new best for me. All of this was an unbelievably emotional time for me. I was always near tears knowing that Dad had "given up" and could be passing away at any moment.

When I got back to Hawthorne that Sunday afternoon, Dad was mostly sleeping, as he had been off water, food, and medication for almost two days. Cheryl had just left, and Rick's family eventually went home that night, but Rick stayed. The next day, September 17, Janet returned from Winters, and Rick left in the evening. Two hours later, Janet and I watched Dad take his last breath.

Even with all we had to do over the next few days, I had a chance to think through what we'd just lost. Not only Dad, but by then we'd also lost the essence of Mom due to her advanced dementia. So much of us comes from our parents. Because sports had always been a major part of our lives, I had grown up on inspirational books they gave me about athletes who defied the odds to become champions. My dad inspired me by attending every Little League game, every Pop Warner football practice and game, and every single high school track meet for four years. During college, he and Mom drove 850 miles round trip for nearly every one of my track meets in Davis over the next four years – just to see a two-minute race and a 50-second relay leg. Mom and Dad taught us everything that's good in people. I didn't work 32 years for the same company without inspiration and guidance from them. I didn't have my wonderful life without their encouragement, devotion, and guidance. And the huge challenge I was to face just two months from then, I could not have managed without being the kind of optimistic person I was because of them.

Lost treasure

The Mercurio family had the funeral arrangements to deal with, Mom to take care of, and facing the future without our patriarch. I don't even want to remember back to those dark days. Since the funeral was set for the end of September, I eventually went home, and Janet had to deal with funeral arrangements and taking care of Mom. I remember writing and placing the obituaries, writing my eulogy (that Katie read for me), finding a donation for mourner contributions, and helping to make decisions about the funeral.

Once the funeral and reception were over, the next weights on our shoulders were Mom and the Hawthorne house. Janet was thinking she wanted to take Mom in and care for her at her house up north, but we all knew that would be virtually impossible for her to pull off successfully. Annette and I had visited a care facility in Simi Valley that seemed perfect for Mom, so Janet called places up where she lived to see if there was a similar home there. She found one, and the decision was made to move Mom there, but all of this was a heavy burden on all of us. Just knowing that both Mom and Dad were no longer in the house they'd been in for 52 years, and that

Mom's functional level was so low she barely knew what was happening, was dreadfully sad.

Janet and I rented a big truck and moved Mom and her belongings to Winters. Janet also took a lot of the furniture to keep herself, including the piano, so when we headed off, the house looked stripped of its character which we all had known for 52 years. It was just another of the non-stop emotional barrages we had to face, and keep going.

The next tragic event for the entire family was losing the treasured Fredalba cabin in the fires in mid October. On October 22, I could see the black smoke from fires to the north and southwest of Simi Valley. During the day on October 23, we got snippets of information about fires in the San Bernardino Mountains, but none seemed close to Fredalba (which consisted of just 19 cabins on a short section of road). It had survived through numerous other forest fires over the years, which approached but never reached The Cabin. This cabin was first bought in 1922 by Mom's aunt. Mom's family spent many wonderful times up there as she was growing up. She and Dad first met there on the July 4th weekend in 1938. When we were kids, we went up there several times each summer.

Eventually, The Cabin was shared by Mom's three Hatch aunts, and in 1962, they had the original cabin torn down and a new one built. This was the cabin where we all had so many memories. My great aunts spent the summers there, and in recent years, so did my aunt and uncle. The entire extended Hatch family visited or used The Cabin frequently. Janet spent her honeymoon there in 1972. We had every Thanksgiving there since about 1973. It was a museum of mementos and antiques from various Hatch relatives who had lived full lives and passed on. There were numerous old photo albums, 19th century marriage certificates, original artwork, old tea sets, antique china and silver sets, 100-yr old books, a National Geographic collection dating to 1915, portraits of our ancestors, the Family Bible with births, deaths and marriages...the list goes on. Eventually, The Cabin had been passed down to Mom and her siblings, and later, Mom had bought out her siblings. Thus, even though it was still used by the entire Hatch/Mercurio family, it belonged to Mom and Dad. We all just assumed it would go on forever when it passed down to the four of us Mercurio siblings.

By Monday, October 24, the winds were howling here in Simi, and we kept hoping that the fires in the mountains would be stopped before crossing the highway into Fredalba. But then we saw bits and pieces of news items that the fires had continued in the direction of Fredalba. For two days on pins and needles, we searched the news reports and online forums to learn the fate of Fredalba, and specifically the fate of The Cabin. We held out a bit of hope that since the siding was asbestos and the roof was metal, maybe it would be spared. No such luck. Rick finally spoke to an LA Times reporter who confirmed that The Cabin was burned completely.

We were all in shock and despair. Nothing left. The extended family was heartbroken, crying. Whereas we knew Dad, Mom, and the Hawthorne home would eventually be gone, we were absolutely unprepared for losing our treasure that we expected to be permanent. (We already had said we would store photo albums and other mementos from the Hawthorne home at The Cabin, so luckily we hadn't already taken those things up there.) It was just so devastating to know that, after 45 years of good times there, I'd never see or be in that cabin again. I drove up there to survey the remains on the first day they let cars up again, and it was surreal to see every cabin in Fredalba burned down to nothing. I took photos and rummaged through for any salvageable pieces, but there was essentially nothing. The fire had completely gutted everything. I did find a few broken remnants to bring home, but they were to show others, not to save.

Rick, Janet and I had to deal with the insurance company for many weeks. We had to document the structures and inventory the contents and their values if we wanted to receive the amount of coverage we had. I started the listing with my estimates, but eventually, Rick handled the structure and Janet the contents, and it took Janet numerous hours to research the value of everything that she and others could remember. I mention this only because the whole tragedy of The Cabin was an ongoing heartache that we had to face immediately following Dad's funeral and in the midst of dealing with the Hawthorne home and getting Mom settled up in the Winters area.

Discovering memories

Just one or two days after we learned that The Cabin had burned down, the four of us Mercurio siblings met in Hawthorne on our pre-arranged date to begin the emotionally difficult task of going through the entire house to make decisions about what to do with everything. This was something we all knew in the backs of our minds we would face some day, but we never let it come to the fore until Dad died. We dreaded it, but knew we had to dismantle where we all grew up, where we continued to visit as our own families grew, and where Mom and Dad lived until the end. Since the house was never remodeled or its contents changed significantly, it was like going through our childhood rooms. We had to take apart our lifelong memories, piece by piece.

However, little did we know the scope of what we would be encountering in old memories and treasures. Yes, we'd all grown up there and had been back constantly over the years since we moved out, but none of us knew the extent to which my parents, mainly Dad, had saved mementos dealing with themselves, us kids, and the six grandchildren. We found Dad's scrapbooks from his childhood, his junior high school yearbooks and certain school work, his high school newspapers, track meet programs from the late 30s (including where Dad competed against Jackie Robinson in the long jump), military records and memos, Hughes Aircraft (his career job) newsletters, Little League programs/newsletters, Pop Warner paraphernalia, tons of our school work, saved newspapers with headlines of momentous events like VE Day, every single Masters Track newsletter for 25 years, every single one of his Corona del Mar Track Club newsletters, his father's mementos, every letter and card they'd received from us over all the years, and I don't know where to end this listing! I've probably remembered only half of the categories of mementos we found.

Much of that weekend was spent finding memories and glorying over them. By the end of the weekend, Cheryl, Rick and I had chosen the few items we wanted to keep for ourselves, and Janet said she'd take the rest. She also volunteered to go through the saved mementos to divvy up items that applied to each of us, like our school work, letters we'd sent them in college, and items related to our own children. Without The Cabin as a storage place any longer, we weren't sure where all the Dad and Mom historical items would go, other than into Janet's basement (the only one of us with a basement or any room for storage).

So, it was an interesting and tough weekend, but the major steps were taken, and only the micro-sorting still needed to be done. As you can imagine, all through October and November there were dozens and dozens of e-mails exchanged among us siblings about what we would do with such-and-such, who wanted what, when we would move things to our own homes, and how much we missed Mom and Dad and our previous way of life as a complete family. It was decided that after Thanksgiving weekend, Janet and I would rent another truck and deliver all of the things that Janet and Cheryl wanted. I would then arrange to have Salvation Army and the trash people come to cart away everything else, and by Christmas, the house would just about be ready to put on the market. It never quite turned out that way, at least not that quickly.

Chapter 13 – On a bike again

Family started arriving for Christmas on Sunday, Dec 23. Instead of the focus being on Dad, Mom, The Cabin, and distributing Hawthorne mementos, much of the attention was on me, which made me feel a bit guilty. I was honestly upbeat, feeling good about my progress and happy to see the additional family members I'd agonized with over the past several months in Redding and Hawthorne.

One positive thing I could do was help take care of Mom. I hadn't seen her since dropping her off in Winters in September. Neither of us could really move around, so we positioned her wheelchair in front of me on the recliner, and I would engage her in conversation ("I use a commode in the bathroom just like you do, Mom. I use a walker just like you do, Mom." Her usual response: "Oh yes, I see that."). Or, the thing we did the most, for seemingly hours on end, was to throw a plastic beach ball back and forth to each other. Mom could still catch and throw, so we just kept up this game to occupy her. Occasionally we'd drop the ball and someone had to retrieve it, but for the most part we just kept tossing.

To accommodate sleeping spots for everyone, we needed to move the motorhome from the driveway into the street. I didn't feel any of us could move the RV except Rick, and he wasn't coming until Christmas Day, so I asked a friend to come do it for me. It worked fine. There I was, outside in my PJs and braces, directing the friend as to where all the ramps needed to go, where to put the rig, and so forth. We were lucky it was warm weather. With so many staying with us, we had people sleeping in the RV, the sofa-bed, the living room couch, and on the floor.

For the big Christmas Eve dinner, the young strong boys carried my recliner chair into the dining room so I could eat with everyone. It was a super dinner, and a good time was had by all. We had appropriate toasts to Dad, Mom, and The Cabin, and then a nice one for me. Everyone else was formal at the table, but of course there I was, set off to the side, holding my bowl up to my face and shoveling in the food.

Christmas morning was very casual, with so many different wake-up times and special needs for Mom and me, that we got started late and without the usual rituals. We got to things when we could, such as grabbing food here and there. We opened the main presents as a group, so that was nice.

By late morning, Katie left to head up to San Francisco with her mom and stepdad, where her fiancé, Jeremy, was waiting. A little later in the day, the Rick clan arrived, for a net gain of five in our house. I was thrilled to have them. Mom and I continued to play ball. Janet had brought mementos from the Hawthorne house, which were upstairs, and I had put The Cabin findings in the garage, so everyone took a turn to go see them.

Before Christmas dinner, Rick and I teamed up to pull my little English Cracker that we all had as favors; when you pull hard and fast, they go "POP." Well, the jolt of the pull hurt my neck. Luckily, it subsided pretty quickly, but that was one of the only times I felt any sharp neck pain during my entire time at home, until I began physical therapy months later. In other words, I was always very protective of my neck!

The crowd pretty much all left the next day. Cheryl stayed one more day, plus Brian was still here. The day after that was my first with my new caregiver, Sandra, from Visiting Angels. She would be spending Mondays through Fridays with me from 9 to 1, every week day until just before my braces came off in mid February. Sandra was originally from Guadalajara, had a 22-yr-old son and two teenage girls.

On that first day with Sandra, she drove me to a local gym and I reached another milestone in my recovery – riding a bike again! This had a huge motivational lift for me, to think I was on the road to normalcy. Dr. Virella had said it was okay to ride a stationary recumbent bike because the back is supported and you sit upright. I was able to leave on the chest brace. So, with much excitement and pride, I pedaled for about 15 minutes that first day, which was a mere 34 days after my accident. I was thinking of the Blue Ridge Parkway. Sandra was thinking I was nuts.

Most significant was the emotional and inspirational triumph this gym visit represented. I was proving I could recover! I was shouting out to the world: "Look at me cycling again! I'm going to do it, folks!"

That was a Friday, and Sandra didn't return until the following Wednesday, January 2, so I had a four-day "recovery" before my next turn on the bike. During the New Year's weekend I proudly shared my cycling progress, always with a lump in my throat.

Chapter 14 – Milestones to normalcy

The new year started with the usual college football games, but the next day started my new routine that lasted until the braces came off on February 19. Annette would help get me up and dressed, get me the paper, and serve me breakfast. Then she'd head off to work and Sandra would come at 9 am. We'd visit for a little while, then go to the gym for my cycling. On returning home, I'd either take a shower or she'd help me clean up with a sponge bath. I took a full shower every other day, still sitting on the commode in the shower with Sandra washing my neck and back, and taking off and then retrieving the braces as needed. Then we'd hang out until noon, when she'd make me lunch. We watched America's Funniest Home Videos almost every day from noon to 1 pm, when she'd leave. In the afternoons I would take naps, work on e-mails, watch the Netflix movies, or read. That was my routine for six weeks.

Sandra also drove me to my many, various medical appointments (except those with Dr. Virella, which was farther away). I had teeth and eye doctors to see because I had been waiting a year for dental and vision insurance to begin in 2008 after a 2007 lapse. I had to get X-rays for an upcoming appointment with Dr. Virella. I developed a bump on my back that kept getting bigger, so I went to the dermatologist to have that removed.

As you might expect, the highlight of my day would be the cycling. It was such a cathartic activity for me, showing me I could be normal again. I kept increasing my time and effort on the machine, and even began doing interval workouts (e.g., 1 minute hard, 1 minute easy, etc.). I eventually got up to about 35 minutes, and could cycle as hard as anyone else there. It was fabulous. Always in the back of my mind was that I needed to keep up the effort if I would ever be able to ride the Blue Ridge Parkway tour in September. Dr. Virella had told me at my January appointment that if all went well, I could ride on the streets again in August. That meant I'd have only five weeks to ride on the roads to train for the very difficult tour, with its 45,000 feet of climbing. Therefore, I had a motivator for riding as hard as I could on the stationary bike.

Sandra and I got to be pretty good friends. We always had a bit of a language barrier, since she'd say things I didn't follow, and I'd say things she wasn't understanding. But all in all, we communicated well enough to converse about family, movies, our backgrounds, and feelings about certain things. She made fun of how skinny I was, calling me Señorito (little man). When washing my back in showers, she would always say "la colita" and laugh, but she refused to tell me what that meant. (I eventually learned many months later that it was a slang term for "little butt.")

Originally, Sandra would give me only small portions of food for lunch, and I'd need to ask her for more. But she eventually caught on and filled me up. I think she had it pretty easy with me compared to her other clients, because she'd always complain about what she had to do for others, and it did sound hard. I thrived on having a companion each day, and when it ended I truly missed it.

Over the weeks I gained the ability to do more and more things on my own. Originally I was instructed not to lift anything over two pounds, but as time went on, I could lift more, which meant I could do some chores. I eventually was able to get my own breakfast, get the newspapers, do laundry, and, thankfully, empty my own urinal each morning. Even though it took forever, I could load and empty the dishwasher one item at a time, bending my entire torso to reach the dishes on the bottom rack. I should note that during my recovery, I got quite good at my peripheral vision, using my sense of feel to find items on the table next to the recliner, and using my toes and feet to get things on the floor. I even mastered changing the toilet-tissue roll with only my right hand and no line of sight (try it sometime, it's tough). I definitely used my grabber too, which clamped items at the end of a 3-foot cane; it really came in handy to pick up all sorts of things, including the clothes from the washer to put into the dryer.

Since I was on pain medication, I suffered the prohibition of any wine or beer. In yet another personal milestone, I was able to wean myself off of the meds by January 10, just 47 days since my accident. Still, it took another couple of weeks, until a visit by Rick in late January, to corrupt me and start me on the "alcohol milestone" to normalcy. Ha! He arrived the night before driving us to our Uncle Dudley's funeral in Hanford (in Central California), and we polished off a bottle of cabernet. After that, I returned to my usual drinking patterns, an obvious demonstration that I was recovering properly!

The ride to Hanford was long, but I had gotten permission from Dr. Virella to loosen the chest brace while driving, so the drive was much more comfortable than previous car rides. They had a touching service for Uncle Dudley (Mom's older brother). Janet brought Mom, so it was nice to get to see her again. I got caught up with many Hatch relatives who had heard only bits and pieces about my accident. There were hours of fond childhood reminiscing at my cousin's afterward, but I missed most of it because the cousins all hung out in the garage while I had to rest inside the house. Thankfully, Rick relayed all the stories and fun on the drive home.

In February, Sarah (brother Rick's daughter) got to stay with us for two weeks during her "externship" at a nearby veterinary clinic. We loved her visit because she is such a fabulous young lady. She jumped right in to help Annette at every chance she got, and was a drinking buddy for me as well. We now know that she made such a good impression on her colleagues there that they made her a job offer she couldn't refuse, to work permanently starting in six more months. Once she and Anthony moved to Valencia in August, we enjoyed having them as our "neighbors."

One day during her two-week stay, Sarah returned to her car to drive home and there was a color flier on her windshield for an all-you-can-eat sushi restaurant. She brought it home, and I got to drooling over it the next day, as it had photos and descriptions of all their special rolls. By the time she returned home that evening, I had circled all the items I wanted, and we agreed to go there for dinner. As Sarah put it, "It would be wrong not to." What a gorge-fest we had! We just kept ordering more and more and kept stuffing ourselves. I actually removed both braces -- the neck so I could chew properly, and the chest for general comfort. We eventually were stuffed to the gills, and we cracked up when I had to put back on the chest brace because it kept popping open. Apparently I had gotten so fat during dinner that the Velcro fastener would not stay closed!

It was about this time that Annette began asking me a question that she repeated every so often until I could think of my answer: Since my life was spared from this terrible accident, she asked, what would I do with my "second chance" to give back and make my life more meaningful? At first I just said I'd have to think about it, which I did. However, I could not think of anything unique that was truly coming from my heart. The thing that kept coming back to me was the symbol of my recovery, the Blue Ridge Parkway ride. I decided that completing that ride might inspire others to overcome their own adversities, and that could be my gift in return for my life.

Chapter 15 – Thorns

Ever since two days after the accident, while I was lying in the hospital bed and my three biking buddies visited, the question of *lawsuit* was brought up. About half the people I would tell about the accident would ask whether I planned to sue the bike manufacturer. I've always had a wariness regarding tort lawsuits because it seems so many of them are frivolous – the victim of an accident just wants someone to blame and wants money. You hear stories of people who just happened to be unfortunate (or were careless) but don't want to take any responsibility, or they want to sting a manufacturer for something outside its true control or liability. Therefore, my first reaction was that I would not bring a lawsuit.

As December wore on, I became aware of expenses I would be facing. Simple out-of-pocket costs, beyond what insurance would cover, might get pretty high. What about a new bike to replace the broken one? Future medical expenses could be significant since I learned that people with fused necks eventually do have vertebrae problems that require medical intervention. My thought was to notify Performance Bicycle about the accident and its apparent cause and see if they would agree to cover these relatively small costs. However, after checking with my legal friends, I learned it's not that simple.

The primary complicating factor is that my health insurance company would be in a position to recover – from *me* – their costs if I was given any money from Performance. So, since my health insurance would likely pay out hundreds of thousands of dollars (which turned out to be true), I would need to get that amount from Performance *plus* the original amount I would seek to cover my relatively small claim. If the amount I'd be asking became *that* high, it was predicted that Performance would never simply agree that their bike had been at fault. They'd have to be "forced" into any sort of payment.

Still, I wanted to at least try to see how Performance would respond to a simple letter that would tell them I'd had an accident; they could come look at the fork, and then we could discuss paying my expenses. So, I called a bike lawyer who advertises not only in *Bicycling* magazine but was a member of the San Fernando Valley Bike Club. He called me back quickly and said he did not do liability lawsuits against manufacturers (he did only legal work involving bikes versus cars), but he recommended a bike lawyer who would. This fellow also called me back quickly and said he would like to see the bike. He drove out a few days later and said it appeared it truly was a product-defect situation, and he figured if I wanted to pursue this, I'd likely prevail. He would agree to write the initial "friendly" letter to Performance, but he predicted, for the reasons mentioned previously, that they would not agree to anything unless "forced" to via legal action.

Sure enough, Performance, in January, responded but only through a law firm they hired; they did not respond as a company. Their legal counsel would view the bike on a specific date in late January at my lawyer's office. My lawyer sent an associate to pick up my bike and all the parts, like the broken spokes, the broken helmet, and the torn clothes. However, Performance's lawyer never showed up at the appointed time. So, my lawyer said we could go ahead and file a suit, which he had said all along would be the only way there would be any meaningful progress. I was torn because if I ever wanted to recover the relatively small portion of money I was seeking, a lawsuit meant I would need to ask not only for the medical costs my insurance would pay, but also a significant percentage more to cover the lawyer's fee. His percentage take would have to be characterized as "pain and suffering" compensation or other probable puffed up reasons, which were claims I just didn't feel comfortable asking for -- at least not the inflated amount I would need to request. (I learned much later that a claimant does not actually sue for a specific amount of damages. It is left completely up to the jury to decide an award. Based on news headlines I'd always seen, I fully believed plaintiffs sued for stated amounts of money.)

With the choice being no action or an action asking for a large amount of money to be able to recover a relatively small amount, I finally did agree to file a lawsuit.

When I originally completed writing this book manuscript in late 2008, very little had happened regarding the lawsuit. The lawyer had only arranged for microscopic analyses of the broken forks and filed subpoenas to the bike manufacturer and to my medical providers. This remained a "thorn in my side" for a long time because it did not come to trial until September, 2009. I have added a Postscript on page 158 describing the trial's outcome.

Another thorn we had to confront was the sale of Annette's old Honda Accord. After we bought her new Accord in late October before my accident, I started advertising the old one on Craig's List and had several inquiries and visits from buyers, but then I had the bike accident. Annette didn't want to deal with potential buyers coming to see it and test drive it, so I just figured it would sit there for a while. But as luck would have it, one potential buyer, who had already test-driven it and made an offer I had refused, called back to see if perhaps it was still for sale and I'd take his original offer. I did, and it was gone. Whew! This thorn we were able to check off the list.

Finally, there was my Bayliner boat I had to deal with. Its engine had failed the previous August at Trinity Lake, and it just sat here at the house for three months waiting until our lives would settle enough for me to take it in for major engine work prior to selling it. I had already decided to sell it, since the annual family houseboat trips appeared to have ended for good. Even if we did continue them, we would prefer renting a ski boat at the lake. So, the plan was to get the boat back running again, and then sell it in the spring when boat sales picked up. Before my accident, I took the boat to a shop in Simi, but when they confirmed it needed a new engine[16], I shopped around on price and

---

16 Letting the boat sit for three months with water in the oil caused everything to corrode internally. Had I not been taking care of my dad

chose a place near Castaic Lake, 36 miles away, recommended by my old mechanic. So, the weekend before my accident, I got out the motorhome and towed the boat to Castaic, figuring I'd be back in two weeks to pick it up again.

Well, you know what happened. When the work was completed, my neck was broken, so we were forced to just leave it at the shop in Castaic. It was always a huge, complicated project to maneuver the boat to the side of the house with only inches of clearance on either side, so I could not ask anyone to do that for me, even if I were directing the process from the sidelines. Luckily, the repair shop owner said he could try selling it for me (for a commission). Since he was the one who had installed the new engine, and he had a lake right there to take potential buyers for test rides, I thought he would be an ideal salesperson. I gave him the go-ahead.

The one thing I still needed to do, however, was to take additional items from the garage that were meant to go with the boat when sold, and, to get things out of the boat that were *not* meant to be sold with it. Remember, when I first took it in for repair, I was not getting it ready for a sale. Therefore, I needed to deliver quite a few things from home to the boat, such as the dinghy, oars, covers, and ropes, and I needed help from someone with a truck to haul all of it. Good old John Bruton to the rescue! We scheduled a day in late January. John got all the things down from the garage rafters, he loaded up his truck, and drove me to Castaic. Afterward, I took John to lunch at a nearby restaurant, and that was the first time I had eaten at a restaurant since my accident. I realized that I had to remove the chest brace and loosen the neck brace to be able to eat, so this was yet another milestone for me. And, it paved the way for the sushi fest with Sarah a week later.

To end the story of the boat, it attracted hardly any potential buyers. The Castaic dealer finally asked me to remove it by April 15 to make way for more repair boats. By then I was able to drive, so I drove the motorhome out there, they hooked it up for me, and I drove it straight to

---

and been able to deal with it within the first few weeks, it could have been fixed for much less.

Ventura to another boat dealer who agreed to try to sell it. A year later with no takers, I brought it home, advertised it on Craig's List for a month, and it finally sold. It took more than 18 months to finally remove that thorn from my side!

Here I am on the ride across the country, in Kansas, about six months before my accident. Notice how I can bend over and use my aero bars with my then-normal neck. (photo by Mike Munk)

I'm feeling the thrill of accomplishment at Salisbury Beach in Massachusetts, at the end of my ride across the country. It was exactly six months to the day before my accident.

Here's my front wheel after the accident, with the fork broken completely in two. A close look reveals half of the spokes missing, since they were instantly sheared off by the upper section of the broken fork blades. This stopped the wheel from turning, which at 28 mph flipped me head-over-wheels onto the roadway.

This shows the upper portion of the sheared-off fork. We learned much later that the fork blades suddenly snapped apart due to poor workmanship, as pockets of air were left in the carbon wraps during manufacture and they grew larger over time, weakening the fork.

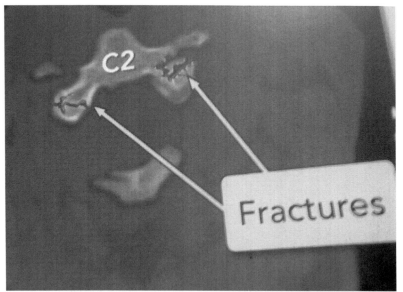

This is an artist's rendering of the CAT scan taken of my neck once I reached the Emergency Room. My C2 vertebra was shattered on both sides surrounding the spinal cord, which lies between those two breaks. The neurosurgeon said after surgery that it was actually much worse than this CAT scan indicated; he said the bone was "pulverized", which led him to suggest it was a miracle that could have happened on both sides of the spinal cord without also injuring it and paralyzing/killing me.

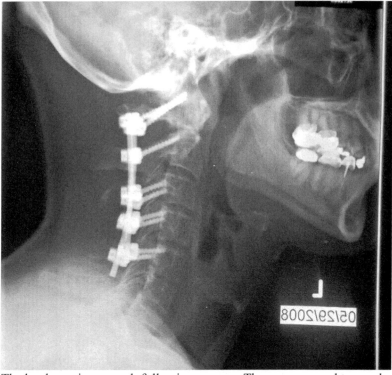

The hardware in my neck following surgery. The surgeon used two rods and all those screws to immobilize my neck for healing, which is also why I will never be able to rotate my head more than a couple inches in any direction. It does not, luckily, set off airport x-ray alarms.

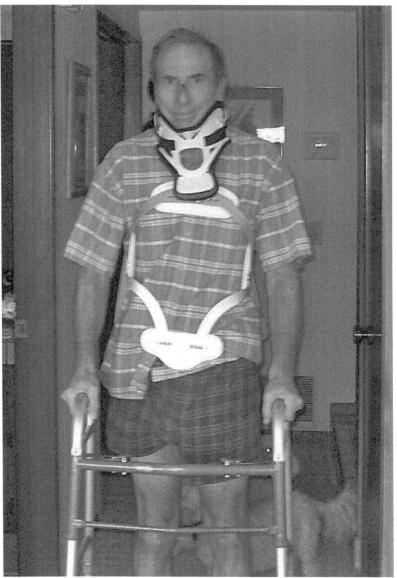

Here I am back home looking happy to be alive. I "suffered" that neck brace and chest brace for three months.

For those three months I spent almost all of my waking hours in this recliner chair in the family room, except when I would be getting my exercise to try to recover as quickly and fully as possible.

I'm with my mom and sister Janet at Mom's care facility in Davis, CA in late spring, 2008 after I no longer needed the braces. I'm glad I got to see Mom then because the next time I saw her in July she had declined with only days to live.

Getting ready for my first bike ride since the accident 6½ months earlier. Only a few minutes before, I had brought my new bike home from the shop. That smile shows my excitement at trying to ride again, but hides my apprehension whether or not I was going to be able to do it.

This is our group of riders at the start of the Blue Ridge Parkway ride in Virginia, September 8, 2008, 9½ months since my accident. I was proud I had made it that far, whether or not I would be able to complete the ride. I am standing 2nd from the left, Bob Brown is to my left, and Bert Stock is standing 2nd from the right. (photo by Curtis Wood)

I'm climbing a hill during the Blue Ridge Parkway ride. Notice my very upright position on the bike, necessary given my stiff neck. I could get no lower on the handlebars, making me quite non-aerodynamic and slow down the hills or into a wind.

I finished! Someone snapped this photo of me with Annette as I had just gotten off my bike at the end of the Blue Ridge Parkway in North Carolina. You cannot tell from this picture, but I was completely overcome with emotion. Triumph!

Chapter 16 – Cycling past 50

When Lance Armstrong won the 1999 Tour de France, it inspired this nation to take up serious cycling. We had had numerous American cycling champions in the past, but theirs were in the days before live TV coverage. Watching the races develop live while listening to the announcers discuss strategies created avid fans of the sport. And the announcers did their best to play up Lance's comeback from cancer, and it inspired us all. Either people were returning to cycling, as with me, or there were greater numbers of new recruits interested in the sport. Each year that Lance won, which was seven in a row, the phenomenon got bigger. I was swept up in this wave.

In the spring of 2000, I decided to ride again in the Solvang Century, a century I'd done many times in the early-mid 80s and once on the tandem (their half-century option) in 1994. I had increased my riding since the previous July when Lance won, and felt I was ready to tackle a century again. It was a great day, and it felt good to be back! I thought I rode reasonably fast, so I was pleased. Another memory I have of that day is that Katie found out she had been accepted to University of Washington, so everyone was celebrating.

The following February, I was now putting in so many miles that I decided it was time for a new bike. Part of the Lance Armstrong Phenomenon was the effect it had on everyone's bike equipment, which was a boon to bike shops and bike manufacturers. We HAD to have the high-tech, light, expensive carbon bikes that the big shots rode, or at least as close to them as we could afford. Besides, since the time of my 1985 Panasonic bike, there were several new features that made bikes safer, lighter, more convenient, and more comfortable. The most significant was that you now shifted near the brake hoods, without having to move your hands off the handlebars nor your eyes off the road. The front crank could be a triple (three different-sized chain rings instead of two), allowing lower gears for easier climbing. Even if the entire bike was not carbon (too expensive), most forks were carbon, meaning the bike absorbed vibrations better for a more comfortable ride. The rear gear cluster had gone from six cogs in 1985 to nine cogs, so again, more gears and therefore narrower differences between each gear for steadier pedaling cadence.

For me, the absolute best improvement was the shoes with cleats that clipped to the pedals. No longer did you need to reach down to loosen your pedal straps when you came to a stop light, and fiddle around when you started up again to get your shoes into the toe cages and then reach down and tighten the straps. That had been such a hassle at every stop and start, and now it was an instant clip-in or clip-out. Yep, had to get me one of those new bikes!

Therefore, just before the 2001 Solvang Century, I bought a new Bianchi Giro from the local All Pro Bicycles in Simi. It had an aluminum frame, a carbon fork, a triple crank and a cluster with 9 cogs in the rear, so 27 gears. I figured with a 4-pound-lighter bike and all the new cool stuff compared to my old bike, and another year of training, I would ride the Solvang 100 miles at least an hour faster than I had the year before. Wrong. I rode a slower time. I *felt* faster, but the clock doesn't lie. Since my new Bianchi had a speedometer/odometer, I could see exactly what my riding time was versus my total time, the difference being the time I was off the bike at the various rest stops. The year before, all I could go on was total time, so I rationalized that maybe I simply spent more time at the rest stops, and that I actually rode faster while I was on the bike. But I was determined, right then and there, that I would be faster the next year in both total time and riding time.

That fall, I decided I wanted to try a multi-day ride. I was always impressed with how the pros in 21-day stage races like the Tour de France could ride over a hundred miles hard every single day, with only two rest days (when they would still ride voluntarily for a couple hours!). I wanted to see if I could ride two or three centuries on consecutive days, so I planned a three-day, 300-mile trip over the mountains to the north, west to the ocean, south to Solvang, and back to the start. I mentioned it to Bob Brown, who had done multi-day trips his entire cycling life, and he suggested I call his friend, Bert Stock (whom I had met years earlier), to see if he would like to join me.

Bert wanted to go but talked me into a two-day ride from his place in Valencia to Carpenteria (south of Santa Barbara) for the first day (85 miles), and back along the coast and through Simi Valley on the second day (90 miles). We had to carry our clothes and toiletries and other necessities in packs, and part of the fun was seeing how little you could manage with since there wasn't much carrying capacity, and you wanted to keep the weight as low as possible. The weather was perfect, and we had a wonderful time. The second day was not bad at all, so I concluded that multi-day rides were do-able. A noteworthy memory from the first night was watching news coverage when the U.S. first attacked Afghanistan just six weeks after 9/11.

The next March, my Solvang Century time was indeed faster than the year before, and I kept pressing on in my new cycling career. With the speedometer, you could monitor your average speed after every ride, and a motivator was to see if you could improve on your speed for any particular course you would ride.

By that fall of 2002, I felt ready to do the three-day ride I had originally planned a year earlier. I again mentioned it to Bob Brown, and he decided he would like to fly out here to do it with me. He then called Bert Stock, and the three of us would go. On a Friday in early November, we departed into the back roads of Southern California.

That first 95-mile day was a heavy day of climbing over the Los Padres Mountains north of Ojai. I assumed we would stop for lunch at the Pine Mountain Inn, which is where we had our lunch break during the Tour of Two Forests double century in 1982, 20 years earlier. I had checked to make sure that the restaurant was still there, so no problem, right? Wrong. It was closed for the winter. I had already run out of water, so I was in bad shape even if the restaurant had still been open. I had "bonked," meaning I was dehydrated, hypoglycemic, and had zero energy. One cannot return to normal simply by drinking or eating; it takes at least until the next day to recover completely. But we absolutely needed water. We had some energy bars and gels to give us some energy, but without water we could not continue at all. As luck would have it, some residents in a trailer saw us milling around the Pine Mountain Inn and asked it they could help us, and they gave us water.

I struggled slowly up the remainder of the climb to the summit, but I was shot. Even down the other side, I was so wasted and going so slowly that Bob and Bert didn't think we'd get to our motel, which was in the middle of nowhere (in New Cuyama if you're familiar with the area), before dark. Fortunately, we came to an unexpected oasis - a bar in a tiny outpost called Halfway Station, where we could eat solid food and get refreshed. After that, I was able to draft Bert into a headwind the remaining 22 miles to New Cuyama, and luckily the longed-for food and drink gave me just enough strength to make it. We got in just before it was too dark to ride. I had the shivers from my bonked-out condition, and remained in my motel bed under all the covers trying to warm up and recover. We eventually ate dinner in their restaurant, and I felt better, but I really needed a good night's sleep.

The next day I felt like a new man, and we rode the 100 miles to Solvang. Did we need to rest after our long ride? No! We went wine tasting with Bert's wife who drove 115 miles there to meet us. The next day we pedaled along Hwy 101 to Santa Barbara and Ventura, and then back to our starting point in a town called Fillmore. The three days totaled 306 miles, and I realized I very much liked multi-day rides, in the back country where it's quiet and scenic (as long as food sources are not unexpectedly closed!). It's you against the elements, which was a challenge I loved.

The next fall, 2003, I did a three-day ride by myself. I started at Rich and Denise Hess' house in Yorba Linda (Orange County), driving there after work on a Wednesday.

Thursday morning I rode down Pacific Coast Hwy to Oceanside, and then inland to brother Rick's house in Valley Center (97 miles that day). The next day I rode 123 miles through touristy Julian, then farther east into the desert, and finally up to Temecula for the night. The third day I rode north and then west back to Rich and Denise's house, for another total of 300+ miles in three days. This time I did it alone, and it felt like a great accomplishment to have made it all by myself. I found too that I enjoyed very much the serenity of quiet roads, the vast scenery to enjoy at my own pace, and the tarantulas crossing the road in the desert.

Therefore, the following year I decided to do another multi-day ride. Where? Switzerland! Of course, I was doing tons of riding all year long, not just in the fall. My interest in cycling just kept getting stronger, and I followed the Tour de France and Lance Armstrong's domination even closer. I gradually understood most of the strategies of stage racing and learned about all the players involved. I had become a cycling nut instead of what I'd been up until then, which was a track and field nut. My cycling fervor continuously became more intense as I got faster, proven each March with speedier Solvang Century times.

But then something occurred that transformed me from a touring-endurance mentality to a race mentality; early in 2004 I bought a book titled, *Cycling Past 50*[17]. From the title, I didn't realize it was all about how to prepare for racing, regardless of age[18]. There were many examples of old timers still racing with fantastic results, and "you can do it too." You just needed to do disciplined interval workouts[19]. I tried to follow the prescriptions in the book, and soon wanted to try out a race.

---

17 Author Joe Friel, published by Human Kinetics, Champaign, IL, 1998.

18 The only thing different for racers over 50 is that we need more recovery time after strenuous efforts. But a publisher knows how to sell books, so they chose a title to capture us boomers who don't want to accept our age.

19 Interval workouts are high intensity with little recovery time between efforts. An example is 10 one-minute intervals with one minute rest between each. Or, three 8-minute intervals at a relatively high heart rate with three minutes rest between each.

Of course, the first thing one "needs" is a new racing bike! So in May of 2004, I bought my Scattante. The model was the CFR, which stood for "Carbon Fiber Racer." But we in the world of food regulatory affairs, my job at Nestle, laughed because our "bible" is the CFR, the government's Code of Federal Regulations. It seemed appropriate that I'd buy a bike called CFR.

Being all carbon, it weighed only about 17.5 pounds. The lighter a bike, the more responsive and faster it is, especially up the hills. And, carbon fiber was said to be stronger than steel and vibration-absorbing. Because my current Bianchi bike was still just fine (with about 17,000 miles on it), I couldn't justify paying thousands of dollars for a new bike...until I saw the Scattante for half the price of a name brand. I figured it was made by the same manufacturer of a name brand, so why pay more? Why pay more? Well, as you know, I would eventually learn the answer to that question the hard way.

I soon tried the Rose Bowl training ride for the first time, and survived my first attempt (that is, I didn't get dropped in the 31-mile "race"). I felt like a full-fledged biker guy. Then in mid June, I drove out to the desert past Palmdale early on a Saturday morning to enter my first honest-to-goodness bike race. It was a 40-km (24-mile) time trial. As soon as I saw the other guys and their bikes, I realized I was in trouble. They all knew each other, they had the expensive time-trial bikes with disk wheels, they were all registered racers, and this, as it turned out, was their state time-trial championship!

For the race, the officials sent us off every 30 seconds, slowest to fastest. Since I had no previous races, I went first in my age 50-60 category. I didn't even have my aero bars yet, which every single time trial rider uses, so I must have looked like a real duffer to those guys. The fellow who started behind me made up his 30-second deficit within about 400 yards. One by one, the 12 other guys in my group sped past me like I was standing still. I fought on anyway, to do my best, and I was properly wiped completely out at the finish line (my butt muscles hurt for days). The other 12 finished between 51 and 59 minutes, and I was 12 minutes behind that! Oh well, my first race was under my belt. And now I at least wanted aero bars.

Once I did get aero bars, which attached to the regular handle bars, I entered several time trials over the next three years on a 20-km course near Piru, a 20-mile drive from Simi Valley. They contest these races monthly, so there are plenty of opportunities to compete. Eventually I was able to win some gold medals in my age category, which was pretty exciting![20] Annette and my parents made quite a thing of that first cycling medal, so I got it engraved with my name, date, and the race particulars.

The only other true race I entered, and the only time I've raced other than in a time trial, was in April, 2006. Five of us Nestle guys decided to try a three-stage race, in which you compete in three separate races over two days; the lowest cumulative time is the winner. The first stage was a 4-mile time trial up a steep road in the Santa Monica Mountains, where I got 9th out of 34. The second stage, later that day, was an 11-mile circuit race (five laps of a course), and I finished in the peloton, so my overall place didn't change. The final stage was the next morning, a 16-mile hilly road race, and I was fifth, moving me up one place to 8th overall. Since my novice category was open to all ages, I was one of the older riders out there; I felt pretty good about 8th versus those younger guys.

Going back to the Switzerland multi-day ride in 2004, it was going to follow a Nestle Regulatory Affairs conference in mid September. I decided to take along my older bike, the Bianchi, and ride for four days in that beautiful, hilly country. I would be planning my route with the Häcki Family the night before I would depart. Annette Häcki was our foreign exchange student for the 97-98 school year, and we have stayed close. Her family lives only about 45 minutes north of where the Nestlé offices are located (which are on Lake Geneva). The conference started on a Tuesday, and that night it rained hard. Everyone got drenched during the long walk from the restaurant to the bus when dinner was over. Once back to my hotel room, I

---

20 It all depended on who showed up the particular day. In the races when I won first place, my time was not necessarily faster than when I got 2nd, 3rd, 4th or 5th.

hung my wet clothes all over the place, wherever I could find a spot. I didn't know then that someone else would need to clean up that huge mess I left in my room. The next morning was "free," whereby we didn't need to show up at the meeting room until 11 am. Big mistake. I spent the early morning putting my bike back together from its carrying case, and decided to take a "test" ride to make sure the bike was right. Once I got outside, however, the weather was super and I just never seemed to want to turn around. I took the road right along Lake Geneva, and pretty soon I was at the east end of the lake going south toward the Rhone River. Eventually I crossed over the Rhone and decided it was time to turn back. I remember thinking that my Swiss biking tour was going to be fabulous if this little excursion was any indication, as I rode through picturesque farming villages and beautiful scenery.

As I got back to Montreux, a few miles before my hotel, I saw a sign for the tiny village of Glion, a picturesque village high up the mountains overlooking the lake. I checked my watch and decided I might have enough time to go up there and still get to the meetings on time. As I headed up the steep hill, I began to question my decision, since it was such a steep hill and was taking a long time. I had 24 miles on my odometer for the ride so far that morning.

Pushing hard, I crept up the grade and finally made it to the quaint little village. I was awed at its incredible views of the lake and Alps, but I immediately needed to head back down the hill because my time was now short. It was so steep that I had to apply the brakes the entire way. The road was shaded and still wet from the rain the night before. Just as I was approaching a hairpin turn to the right, a car needed to pass me, the only car that had been on that road in many minutes. After the car passed, I had to swing back out to the middle of the road to have more room for my turn, but then I was suddenly in the turn and needed to lean far to the right to negotiate the hairpin. I had not properly slowed enough, and with the pavement slick from the rain, I was down before I knew what happened.

I hit the ground hard on my right hip and helmet and did not skid at all. That is, the entire force from my weight and my speed had gone into the impact on my hip. It hurt BAD. I couldn't move my right leg at all. And there I lay in the middle of the road with no one around. I finally decided it might be best to get out of the road, so I pulled myself to the curb, dragging the bad leg. Man, the pain was excruciating! Even as I lay there in extreme pain, it's funny that thoughts immediately went through my head about whether I'd still be able to do the planned tour ride in a few days. Is that "funny," or is it "sick"? Maybe it *is* bizarre, but that same attitude is apparently what drove me to recover as fully as possible after breaking my neck. Never say die!

Pretty soon a car came down the hill, and the guy stopped and said something to me in French, and I said something in English, and he pulled out his cell phone. Then I knew this would be big. A few residents from the nearby homes had come out to see me by then, and next I heard a siren. It got closer and closer, and the rest is history. I had a broken hip, they operated on me later that afternoon, I stayed in the Montreux Hospital with a view of the Alps for three days, and then recuperated at the Häckis for a week. I became infamous around Nestle for riding a bike and breaking my hip during a company conference.

A brief story about my broken hip demonstrates again how I was one fortunate soul on the right side of luck. My break was at the femoral neck, where the femur connects to the ball of the hip joint. The surgery was straightforward - they inserted three screws from the side to reconnect the break which was completely through the bone. In 50% of patients who suffer this break, the blood supply to the hip is lost resulting in the need for a hip replacement. This is exactly what happened to Floyd Landis, who won the 2006 Tour de France (but lost it due to doping). He broke his hip exactly where I did (from a bike fall exactly like mine) and underwent the same surgery, but he wasn't so lucky and he had to get a hip replacement. The anxious thing is that you must sweat out for many months before knowing whether you've lost your blood supply or not[21]. It was a

---

21 In fact, prior to my surgery that afternoon in Switzerland, the doctor told me about this 50-50 chance that the surgery would be unsuccessful, and

great relief around Christmas time when we could finally conclude I was going to be okay.

I walked on crutches for eight weeks, was back on the bike before Christmas, and was riding full bore by February. Then I broke my fibula bone in my left ankle when I fell on black ice while visiting Brian in Columbus in early February. With determination to recover as soon as possible, I rode in the Solvang Century a month later on the very day after the doctor said I could discontinue using my foot brace. The following October I had the three screws in my right hip removed, and the leg has been like new ever since. Both broken bones are just a distant memory.

In November 2005 and 2006, I took the motorhome to Solvang for four days and did different long rides each day. It was always perfect weather and I had a wonderful time seeing the countryside and vineyards (and Michael Jackson's Neverland from a hillside above it). In May of 2005 I did the Davis Double Century, and finished in a respectable time of 15 hours. It was a chore over the last 40 miles, and I got a bit sick to my stomach. I decided never to do a double again; regular centuries (100 miles) would be fine for me at my age. (Well, that resolution didn't hold up as it turned out.)

I rode and rode and rode, always getting better and looking for the next challenge. It would come when I retired from Nestlé in September, 2006.

---

asked if I would like a hip replacement instead. Fortunately, I chose the simpler option that day.

Chapter 17 – Shedding the hardware

Three months after my neck surgery, I was anxious beyond belief to get both of my braces off for good. I was sick and tired of those "little prisons." The doctor had said three months, which would be February 24, but I was pushing to see if I could shed my braces at 12 weeks. What's the difference? Well, 12 weeks *sounds* like three months, but it's actually a week earlier, and even one *hour* earlier would be a blessed pardon. So, my doctor appointment to assess my readiness was set for Friday, February 15, two days shy of 12 weeks since the surgery. A few days prior to the appointment, I went in to get the prescribed X-rays. This time, the doctor had asked for X-rays of my chest as well as my neck, to see whether my thoracic vertebrae had healed.

When I picked up the X-rays, there was included a written report to Dr. Virella from the radiologist. It sounded as if my neck was fine, but his description of my back made it sound like I was ready to sit in a wheelchair the rest of my life. It mentioned several problems he had found, and I became suddenly very worried. However, when I gave Dr. Virella the X-rays and written report at the appointment, all he could say was, "Where are the flexion and extension pictures?" Huh? I told him that what he had were all they took. He checked back in his file and sure enough, he said, he had forgotten to ask for X-rays to be taken as I was extending my neck downward and flexing it back as far as I could. Therefore, he said, I could dump the chest brace, but I would need to wait until they took the two additional neck X-rays before I could remove the neck brace.

Well, that was good news to an extent, since the chest brace was a far bigger bother than the neck brace. But darn, now I had to wait longer for complete freedom. And what about the radiologist's report about my "serious" new back problems? I cracked up because Dr. Virella just brushed it off, saying those radiologists are just picky and try to point out everything regardless of its importance. "Do you have any back pain?" he asked. "No," I answered. "Okay, don't worry about it." Whew, what a relief!

Dr. Virella knew I was anxious to get rid of the remaining neck brace and begin physical therapy, so he said I could get the two missing X-rays on Monday, they could fax him the results, and I could call him on Tuesday, February 19, to get his answer. He also wrote me the prescription for physical therapy assuming the X-rays would clear me. It all worked like clockwork, except for Dr. Virella returning my phone call on Tuesday to give me the good news I wanted. Finally, at about 4 pm, I called his office again. The receptionist asked me to hold while she went to ask him. I waited with bated breath... I waited...I know neither she nor Dr. Virella knew how anxious I was waiting for a positive answer, so it was pretty funny when finally she came back to the phone and made it sound like it was no big deal: "He said you can stop wearing the brace." To me that was like VE Day, but I just thanked her calmly and proceeded to scream for joy inside.

I immediately called Annette, but had to leave a message. Funny, but in the middle of my message, I realized that in my exhilaration I had forgotten yet to actually remove the brace that I was so anxious to be rid of!

Intermixed with this achievement for me was sadness for our dog Becky. Three days earlier, the day after I got to remove the chest brace, Becky began to get sick; she couldn't eat, she coughed and gagged a lot, and was listless most of the day. It worsened the next day (Sunday), and Annette sat next to her as she slept and lay there in obvious discomfort. By Monday morning, February 18, my caregiver and I took her to the vet and left her for testing and observation. The vet called later to say Becky would not recover and recommended we put her to sleep. Annette came home from work early, and we went to the vet's office to see her one last time and have it done. As you would know, this was extremely difficult, especially for Annette to lose the friend she loved so much. Annette cried and cried and reminisced the entire evening and for weeks after. We created some written memories and got a special box to put a few mementos in. What a roller coaster ride emotionally to have Becky die just as I was celebrating getting rid of my braces.

Once I was free of the braces, I could finally start on my road to recovery with physical therapy. The first question was: Which physical therapist? I had two issues to contend with: 1) I needed to find a PT who accepted my insurance, and 2) I wanted to find one within walking distance since my caregiver coverage from my insurance ended the day I could stop wearing the braces. So, on that same Monday the 18th when Becky died and I got my additional neck X-rays, I looked in the phone book for PTs. One was listed in the office buildings that sat only 200 yards across the park! Would I have another stroke of luck in this saga, that they would accept me and my insurance company, and I wouldn't need taxi rides to get to my appointments? I walked over there, gave them my prescription and my insurance card, and they said YES! How about that? Only a couple hundred yards to walk; I couldn't believe my good fortune.

A fourth major event for Monday the 18th was my final visit to the gym to ride the stationary bike. An interesting side story is that the caregiver by now was no longer Sandra. Within the previous one week, I had a total of four different caregivers. The Monday before, Sandra had arrived with a bad cold. She kept insisting that she'd be okay, so right away we went to the gym as usual, where she kept sneezing and blowing her nose. When we returned, I insisted she go home immediately and get better, which she did. The next day, Visiting Angels called to say that Sandra was still sick, so a woman named Danielle would come.

What a difference Danielle was! Whereas Sandra and I conversed only superficially due to the language barrier, Danielle was an engaging conversationalist, wanting to know everything about everything. She also was a bit of a philosopher, faith healer, and spiritual guru. Our conversations went in all directions, and we liked each other. She also claimed to have been a massage therapist once in her life, so I let her work on my back, head, neck, and feet. It was marvelous. She gave me a list of inspirational movies I could watch (which I did), and kept telling me she could "see" in me that I would have a changed life once I was recovered. I now believe she may have had some psychic abilities, because my life has indeed become richer as I have explored and begun to blossom spiritually.

The next morning, I was looking forward to Danielle returning, but a new caregiver was at the front door. It turned out that Danielle had gotten a new job after leaving here the previous day, so Visiting Angels needed to find yet another caregiver for me. Jasmine, an actual Registered Nurse, and I got along great too, again with the conversation going in all directions. She was the only caregiver to exercise at the gym alongside me. We watched a movie and had a lot of fun over the next three days, leading up to my big Friday to see Dr. Virella about shedding the braces.

By the following Monday, however, they sent yet another caregiver, whose name I don't remember. She spoke very little English, actually, and we did not talk much. She's the one who drove me for the X-rays, to the vet, and to my final visit at the gym. To have special fun, before going to the gym I decided to go to the bakery at the mall where the San Fernando Valley Bike Club stopped every Monday on their informal rides. It was a hearty boost to get to see so many of my biking buddies again, and have them congratulate me on my progress. I promised them I'd be back with them soon, although I didn't know that for sure. After visiting with the bike club, I made that final visit to the gym to ride the stationary bike. By then I could ride pretty darned hard and long, lifting my spirits to know I was truly recovering.

What a week that had been, but now a new phase of my recovery would begin!

Chapter 18 – Gaining strength

Without the braces, I began a new life of stationary cycling, physical therapy, and walking.

One of the first happy moments I got to realize, however, was getting to take a normal shower again. By myself. Standing up instead of sitting. No ladies looking at me. In our master bathroom, not downstairs. Ahhhh, a regular shower! And using the regular toilets instead of the portable commode. It's funny how little things like a shower can have such a big impact on making you feel like you're going to be your old self again.

I couldn't wait to start riding my real bike on the trainer, since that would simulate riding on the street better than riding the stationary recumbent at the gym. It took me a few days to get up enough confidence that I could lift the Bianchi bike off its hooks in the garage and position it into the trainer, but I did. I savored the moment when I conquered one more demon by climbing on a bike for the first time since November 24.

Riding the bike was not difficult, except to the extent of how hard I would elect to push myself. Although my neck and back were always stiff and sore, at least they were okay as it related to pedaling the bike. Of course, I couldn't bend my neck upward enough to see above my front wheel, and that scared me. I just had to hope that my physical therapy would increase my range of motion to solve that problem. In the meantime, I looked downward as I pedaled, and I could ride as hard as I wanted. I decided to ride every other day, and the days in between would be for walking to give me weight-bearing exercise to help with the bone formation in my neck.

I knew I would be using a trainer exclusively for a long time – 5½ months. And I knew I would need to train hard on it if I was going to be able to prepare for the Blue Ridge Parkway ride. Unfortunately, it's very boring to just pedal in place, looking at the same ground underneath your bike the entire time. And you just drip sweat, which necessitates a towel be draped along the top tube of the bike. Sometimes I set up a fan to blow on me, if my workout would be long or especially strenuous, and that helped with the amount of sweat. At first I could ride hard like that no longer than 20 minutes, but that worked up to 30 minutes, and eventually, when I did interval workouts, I was in the saddle for just over an hour. Also, after a few weeks I wised up and moved the bike and trainer to the back yard, to drink up the beauty of our garden while pedaling and "dreaming of glory."

Physical therapy was the next biggest part of my days. I went three times a week for about an hour. The PT was fine, but his assistant was a real hoot. She teased everyone, and I laughed all the time at the banter back and forth between her and the clients. I took her a Dear Abby headline that I had found saying, "Veronica is mean, and she needs to know it." She proudly posted it for all to see, and it remained up the rest of my time there.

At first they had me lift 1-lb weights, over my head and side to side. Eventually I would get up to 15 lbs, but I sure felt like a weakling when I started. To increase my range of motion, I'd stretch my neck side to side and up and down. I was supposed to do this at home too, and I did so faithfully. I kept picturing that I'd need the side-to-side mobility to be able to drive again and the upward mobility to bicycle again. With those goals in mind, I'd push through the pain twice a day, 10 times in each direction. The therapist had said early on that he doubted I'd ever get an upward range of motion sufficient to ride a bike again, but I wanted to prove him wrong.

To help my stiff back and ease the pain I endured when walking long distances, they had me lie on a towel roll about five inches in diameter, placed under my back, and stretch my arms backward behind me 10 times. It really hurt at first, but over time it got to feeling good. I could feel and hear the bones cracking, as when someone cracks his knuckles. I have continued to do this towel-roll stretching several times a day to the present time.

Speaking of bones cracking, the physical therapist would spend about 10 minutes of each session manipulating my head in various directions as I lay on my back. Every so often, as he'd turn my head to the left or right, there'd be a loud CRACK in my neck. It scared the heck out of me whenever it happened, but the therapist said it was a good thing. Still, I would resist after it happened, because in my mind, it seemed like I had just broken something.

Walking. Once I was without a caregiver to drive me, I walked and walked all over town. To the bank (3 miles), to the post office (2 miles), to the dry cleaner's (1.2 miles), to the grocery store (1 mile), to the bookstore (1 mile), and even to the vet to pick up medicine for Lily (5 miles). I knew it was good for me, so I tried to walk somewhere every day. However, my upper back, just left of center, would always hurt badly. Sitting for a few minutes would help ease the pain for a little while, but it would always return when I continued walking.

I do believe that the back pain I experienced was severe enough that it would have forced most people to avoid walking very far at all. Again, my motivation pushed me beyond what I think was the norm. I was determined to withstand whatever discomfort and pain I faced, to recover as fully and as quickly as I could. Without the Blue Ridge Parkway goal, I think I still would have been motivated to heal as much as I could and would have walked some, but I doubt I would have pushed myself as extensively and consistently as I did.

The other thing missing once the caregivers stopped coming, besides being driven around, was social interaction during the days. I had a little bit at the physical therapy appointments, but I reached out for more. I walked to the hospital to see if I'd recognize anyone, and I did see Melissa, the physical therapist. We chatted for a few minutes and it was fun to discuss my progress. When I got home I decided to call and see if she wanted to visit longer, such as over lunch. She agreed, but I could sense some reluctance. Over the next two months, I enjoyed lunch with her in the hospital cafeteria four times, and I think she was okay with it. She and her fiancé had gone to U.C. Davis, so we had that in common. She was getting married in July, and Katie was getting married in May, so we had that in common. She reminded me of some of the funny stuff that happened while she was helping me get out of bed and learning to walk. Her funniest memory was how excited I was when she showed up one day so she could help me get to the bathroom for a "desperate" visit.

I also popped in twice on our next-door neighbor, saying "I thought I'd be neighborly and see if you wanted to visit for a little while." Once I walked to the theater to see a movie with friend Barbara.

One day in late March I decided to see if I could mow the lawns again. My biggest concern was whether I could pull hard and fast enough on the cord to start the engine, since it could be quite a jolt to my neck. I started gradually to see how it would feel, and of course it was not near enough to start the engine. But, increasing my efforts didn't seem to hurt my neck, so eventually I could pull fast enough and it started. After that, it was "no sweat" just to push it around the lawns. Annette had a fit that evening when she realized what I'd done, but just sighed and figured she couldn't stop me from trying to get back to normal. I *was* going to get back to normal!

One of the funniest stories was when I decided to go visit my bike shop. I knew the folks at All Pro Bicycles since I had been in that store so many times and bought so much stuff there, including my Bianchi bike. As I walked in the door, co-owner Gina asked how I'd been. I said I was recovering from a broken neck, and when she asked me what happened, I said, "Well, last November my fork broke while..." That's all the farther I got in my reply, because all four people in the store turned at that moment and said, almost at the same time, "That was YOU?"

They all had heard about someone who had a bad accident because of a broken fork, but they hadn't known who it was. Thurlow Rogers was one of the people in the shop[22], and of course he was the ride leader that day I fell.

---

22 I had seen him there occasionally before my accident, but I understood he was just helping out sometimes. However, at some point, he became

Everyone stopped what they were doing to get all the details of what happened and how I was. We joked that it was Thurlow's fault for pulling the group at such a fast speed. They also teased me about riding an off-brand bike and admitted that they had wondered about that bike when I brought it in for servicing. I visited the bike shop two other times, showing everyone my X-rays on the next visit. Dave, the other co-owner, kidded that if I had a neck problem in the future, I should go to a hardware store, not a doctor, with all that metal in my neck.

It was about that time when I decided to write this book. We were having dinner with John and Lynn Bruton, and although John had been around here for all the stories about my accident, Lynn hadn't[23]. So, she kept asking us details about what happened and how we felt, and finally John said, "Why don't you just write a book?" He wasn't serious, and I laughed it off. Even if he had been serious, I would have dismissed it. However, over the next few days I kept thinking about it. Then suddenly while walking on our treadmill upstairs, a title and a first sentence came to me. I thought they sounded funny, and from there I started typing away.

---

a regular employee and I bought stuff from him. For me, it was like buying a Dirty Harry video at Blockbuster directly from Clint Eastwood. I was too star-struck to say anything special to him. But, I eventually told everyone that I bought my new bike shoes from Thurlow Rogers, and they were duly impressed.

23 John and Lynn used to live in Simi Valley, but moved to Chicago in 2005 for Lynn's job. However, John continued his professorship at Cal State Northridge, so during teaching times, he lived in an apartment in Simi Valley. On this occasion, Lynn was visiting here.

Chapter 19 - Just tie me to a chair in the house

Dr. Virella originally said that once I started PT, I might be able to drive a car again in one month. As it turned out, I didn't feel ready when a month had gone by. I just couldn't move my neck enough to the left and right. However, after six weeks, I felt it could be okay. Plus, at a Chinese restaurant, the fortune in my cookie had been, "Your place in life is in the driver's seat." That *obviously* meant it was destined to be, so I scheduled an appointment with Dr. Virella, who did indeed give his approval to drive. Interestingly, he didn't independently test my neck's range of motion as we thought he would. His test of my readiness was simply to ask this question: "Do you think you can drive safely?" Hahaha. Of course, he also gave me his usual reminder -- how lucky I was to have survived my bike accident. Amen!

Well, getting to drive again would be HUGE! More than anything else, this would allow me to live a normal life again. It also meant I could drive myself in the motorhome the following Monday, April 7, for the third annual spring fling at Uncle Ed's[24] instead of making Rick come out of his way to Simi to drive me there. It was a Friday afternoon when I left Dr. Virella's office with this great news, and on the drive home, while Annette drove since I didn't yet have blind-spot mirrors, I phoned family and friends to tell them. Then I e-mailed dozens of people with the heading "I can drive again." I even promised several Nestle people that I would finally drive in to work the following week for my

---

24 Uncle Ed is Beth's brother who lives a "survival life" out in the desert east of Apple Valley with his wife. Rick and a few of us enjoyed "guy" weekends there once a year, mostly drinking beer and philosophizing!

first visit with them since the accident. As it turned out, I was jumping the gun.

First I needed the blind-spot mirrors for my car. So, I phoned John Bruton to arrange for him to drive me, in my car, to the auto parts store. The next morning I pulled my Toyota Camry out into the driveway and gave it a thorough cleaning, inside and out, since it had been just sitting for several months. John came at the appointed time, and off we went to the store. Not only did I buy the mirrors, but an oil filter.

I would never need that oil filter. On the return trip, with John still driving since I was planning to put on the mirrors back at home, WE GOT IN A CAR CRASH! Can you believe it?? As we were driving down a four-lane road, a car that had been on the right waiting for us to pass her so she could make a U-turn, made her U-turn right into us! It turned out she didn't see us, even though it sure seemed like she was waiting for us. Anyway, she hit us pretty hard on the right, but luckily behind me, and it spun us around. If she had started her turn a split second sooner, she would have hit right into me. Again, if I had to have bad luck, it was associated with good luck. My blessings were never-ending. I think my Fathers were on their couch again watching my adventures on their big-screen, ready to lend a helping hand.

There was my car, spun around facing the wrong direction, parts broken off banging in the street, and a crowd forming instantly (where did all these people suddenly come from?). This was a major crash scene! Interestingly, I didn't even think about my neck at first. I felt fine. You'd have thought that being in a car crash like that would have jerked my neck, but it hadn't. Apparently, getting hit on the side near the back of the car allowed the force of her impact to spin us rather than apply a direct jolt to John and me. Also, since she was just starting her U-turn, she wasn't going very fast yet. Again, if I had to have the bad luck of a serious car crash, it was associated with the good fortune of not getting hit straight from behind or us hitting straight into someone else, which would likely have sent me off to the Emergency Room for a new neck surgery, and who knows what else? I'm lovingly watched over or just a lucky stiff – you decide.

My car was inoperable. The right rear wheel and axle were bent. John quickly went to ascertain the condition of the other driver, who was okay. I slowly got out of the car, and went to the sidewalk. The police were there already! Later, even a fire engine and an ambulance came. We were a hot item! As the police were questioning us, one of them remembered me from my bike accident, lying there on Los Angeles Avenue. He asked how I was doing, but little else. I guess he didn't think it was as coincidental as I did.

Eventually the tow truck took my Camry to the local body shop, and we needed a ride home. Annette was away at a meeting, so I couldn't call her, and most of our other friends were at the same meeting. John was able to contact his old next-door neighbor, who graciously drove us to my house. John and I promptly got in his truck and went out to eat. The whole thing was a bit surreal to me. Here I could finally drive, but now I had nothing to drive! I was in a "serious" car accident, but everyone was fine and we were at a restaurant as if nothing had happened. The stories never seemed to end for me. Everyone was astounded at all that had happened, and at my good luck in spite of bad luck.

I did have the motorhome, however. I could still drive that, and it even already had blind-spot mirrors! So, I did get to drive out to Uncle Ed's on Monday, and it felt liberating to be able to drive again and be independent. I had to turn my torso to the right to be able to see out the right mirror, but twisting my entire upper body right or left to see sideways was simply my new way of life. I was sooooo careful when first I drove, checking the mirrors almost constantly and poking along below the speed limit, never wanting to change lanes. That first drive was in light traffic, which allowed me to gain confidence.

We had a great two days at Uncle Ed's, playing poker almost the entire time and watching some movies. I was on the phone with the car insurance people quite a bit, trying to straighten them out that although I wasn't driving when the accident happened, I was the owner of the car; they kept getting that wrong. The fling soon ended and I drove back home.

You'll never guess what happened next! The following day, a Wednesday, I decided to take care of a little chore. In January I had received a Ford recall notice asking me to take the motorhome to a Ford dealer for a quick replacement part. I never could drive it until now, so I decided that while the motorhome was out on the street (not stored next to the house that was tricky to retrieve and put away), I could get that little issue taken care of. As I had done the previous Saturday with my Camry, I first gave the motorhome a good washing (a lengthy and difficult chore with a huge RV and a stiff neck). After what happened to my newly cleaned Camry, I should have figured something was going to go wrong with my brand-clean motorhome.

After the washing, I drove the RV to the Ford dealer and waited the 30 minutes while they did their fix. But then they approached me and said, "We'll pay to repair it, but we damaged the back end of your rig." WHAT? Sure enough, when they were done with their repair, one of their workers backed it into a brand new truck sitting behind it. Can you believe it? All I could do was laugh.

We called an RV repair shop, and I drove it there while the Ford man followed me. After leaving the motorhome, the Ford man drove me home. When I came in the house, I had such an empty feeling. Within five days of getting approval to drive, both my vehicles were in body shops. When John Bruton told his wife Lynn about this recent setback, she said that someone needed to tie me to my chair and not let me out of the house! Everyone who heard my crash stories had a similar reaction. What in the heck was going to happen NEXT?

I got word two days later that my Toyota would be considered a total loss. Pretty terrible, right? Well, not so fast. In yet another example of making lemonade from lemons, before the car accident I already was wondering if I would need a car with an automatic transmission, since it might have been impossible for me to have pushed in a clutch with my left foot while trying to turn my body around to the left to look behind me. So, as the week wore on, I was actually hoping the car would be considered a total loss so that not only could I get a new one with an automatic, but I could get one quickly and finally begin driving. When that happened, I happily looked at used-car ads, and on Sunday of that same week I bought a 2002 Mitsubishi Galant from the local Simi Toyota dealer. I eventually got from the insurance company what I felt was a fair price for the Camry and had no deductible since it was the other driver's fault. The Galant seemed like a new luxury car compared to the old '96 Camry, and it was only a few grand more than what the insurance paid me.

Before I could drive the Galant home from the dealer, we had to put on the blind-spot mirrors that I had purchased the Saturday before. Finally I could drive a car again! The feelings of freedom I had earlier in the week in the motorhome were realized again, and it was great on that short drive home. I did have to get used to using the little blind-spot mirrors and turning my whole body when in tight quarters or at intersections, but that all came quickly.

I now had my new car in time to drive to Costa Mesa to see the America By Bicycle staff as they were getting ready for the 2008 ride across the country. It was fun seeing them again and comparing stories from the past year. The tour leader had ridden on the Blue Ridge Parkway and said it was one of the hardest rides he'd ever done because of all the climbing. He laughed when he thought of me having only five weeks to ride on the streets to prepare for it, but also didn't want to blatantly discourage me, so he did his best to say positive things about my chances.

My car also gave me the freedom to finally visit my Nestle friends. I took along my visual aids – my X-rays – as they always impressed everyone. Some people thought I was nuts to want to cycle again, but I was getting that from about half my friends and relatives anyway, so I was used to it. I noticed that most men supported my getting back on the bike, while most women wanted to tie me to a chair.

Being able to drive was a milestone that truly did make me feel like I was normal again. Now all that was left was seeing if I could ride a bike on the streets.

Chapter 20 – No more singing the national anthem

As if my stiff neck weren't enough, I developed two health annoyances. One of those is still with me and likely always will be, and actually is more than just a health issue.

The first occurred in March when I noticed that my elbows became sensitive and would hurt if I bumped them into something or pressed them down against a hard surface. I didn't think much of it until one elbow developed a big puffy fluid pocket around it. I went to see my orthopedic surgeon who said it was a separation of the tissue from the bone, and that it happened when I had my accident. He didn't think it was serious and would normally do a quick surgery to fix it, but said he should wait until my neck was better. He gave me a little white cushion-pad to wear over the elbow.

Interestingly, while the fluid pocket gradually subsided after about six weeks, the same thing developed on my other elbow! Then I was wearing *two* white elbow pads, which I continued to wear for several months until both elbows healed up on their own.

Then, beginning in May, I began to have a problem swallowing my larger pills. They would get stuck halfway down in my throat. At first, a couple extra big swallows would get them to continue on down my throat. But then that stopped working, and I'd need to eat something solid to get them to continue down. Finally, even that didn't work, and the pill would sit there in the middle of my throat for minutes until something, drinking or eating, would finally dislodge it.

Since I'd already had concerns about my throat, I decided to ask Dr. Virella about it. After the accident, I never did get my normal voice back, as I was a little raspy. Plus, I couldn't sing anymore, at least not beyond a single octave of the scale. I thought I might get my singing ability back if the tightness in my neck dissipated, but the tightness never went away (and never will). Thus, by May I hadn't seen any improvement at all in my singing or my raspiness.

Losing my ability to sing was a major disappointment and a source of ongoing sadness. I considered myself a pretty decent singer. I've sung all my life, and think of singing as one of life's greatest pleasures. Ever since I was 20, I'd played piano and sung songs, mostly for myself but sometimes for others as well. I occasionally did karaoke performances. I sang in the Nestlé Choir, and we recorded a CD. I sang the pre-game National Anthem in Dodger Stadium! (Okay, okay, I was part of a Nestlé quartet, not a soloist, but still!) I sang with the Nestlé Choir in Staples Center before a Clippers game. It hurts inside to not be the singer I once was. Luckily, I can still sing (with a raspier voice) as long as I'm within my octave range; however, jumping up and down octaves to be able to cover a song's scales is unnatural and annoying.

Additionally, just the process of swallowing felt tight and different, and I would occasionally choke and cough while drinking or eating. Dr. Virella said he'd never heard of someone's throat being impacted like this after my type of surgery, so he referred me to a gastroenterologist. That doctor put a scope down my throat and said everything basically looked fine, but it was a little red, so maybe I had Laryngopharyngeal Reflux. Huh? This is when acid from the stomach comes back up to the throat and irritates it. Why would I have this? He didn't know but could only guess that due to my old age (!), my sphincter where the esophagus enters the stomach had become defective. He decided to prescribe Nexium, which inhibits acid being pumped into the stomach.

Well, the next two months of dealing with this issue were a major aggravation. I think I would just as soon have had my swallowing problems than having to deal with fixing them, as it turned out. First, the problem with taking Nexium was you had to take it first thing in the morning and then wait an hour before eating or drinking anything else. Second, if I really did have Laryngopharyngeal Reflux, I wasn't supposed to eat anything three hours before lying flat, such as going to bed. Finally, and worst, I was not supposed to drink alcohol, orange juice, lemonade, caffeine, or cola beverages, and I was to avoid eating spicy foods, cheese, fried foods, eggs or chocolate. Talk about ruining my life as I knew it! Those were the only things I ate or drank, it seemed like. Jokingly, I asked myself: What was the point of my throat getting better if this was going to be my new life?

I wanted to follow all these rules because the online information on Laryngopharyngeal Reflux said that it can also cause raspy voice and impact your singing, so I believed I must have had it and wanted my singing to get back to normal. But oh did I dislike those restrictions! At Katie's wedding, I decided to go ahead and have some champagne for the toasts, but the rest of the time I was "suffering" a bland life.

Luckily, when I saw the doctor for my one-month check and complained about my insipid lifestyle, he freed me! He said that because I was taking Nexium, it allowed me to "cheat" to an extent. That was because the acid that all those prohibited drinks and foods created in the stomach was being inhibited by the drug. I shouldn't overdo it, he said, but I could have some of all those verboten foods. (I sure wish doctors would fully explain these sorts of things initially, instead of simply handing you a sheet of paper with instructions that do not fully apply to your situation.)

Suddenly my life was good again. And, it got even better as I began to rationalize that I probably didn't have Laryngopharyngeal Reflux in the first place. The pill swallowing hadn't gotten any better (so I had decided simply to avoid big pills), my raspy voice hadn't changed, my singing hadn't improved, and many health professionals had told me "*Of course* your throat problems are from the surgery! Your neck has been significantly altered, and your throat is part of what's been changed." They were surprised the two doctors hadn't come to the same conclusion.

So, I figured I didn't have this big-named problem after all, and I pretty much went back to my normal diet. I continued taking the Nexium until my two-month visit with the gastroenterologist, when even he agreed that since it hadn't helped anything, I probably never had the acid reflux malady in the first place.

So, what were/are these throat maladies related to? Dr. Virella had said he had no idea, and that they were certainly not from anything related to his surgery. However, I now question that. A few years after my surgery, Annette heard that the "high tech" protein, BMP or Bone Morphogenetic Protein, which Dr. Virella applied during surgery to stimulate my new bone fusion, was found to be potentially harmful. I immediately did an Internet search, and sure enough, the FDA issued a warning Notification on July 1, 2008, that BMP should NOT BE USED in the neck for spinal surgeries. Whoa!

The FDA Public Health Notification began this way:

"Dear Healthcare Practitioner:

"This is to alert you to reports of life-threatening complications associated with recombinant[25] human Bone Morphogenetic Protein (rhBMP) when used in the cervical spine. **Note that the safety and effectiveness of rhBMP in the cervical spine have not been demonstrated and these products are not approved by FDA for this use.**

"FDA has received at least 38 reports of complications during the last 4 years with the use of rhBMP in cervical spine fusion. These complications were associated with swelling of neck and throat tissue, which resulted in compression of the airway and/or neurological structures in the neck. Some reports describe difficulty swallowing,

---

25 Recombinant means it was made using modern biotechnology genetic techniques.

breathing or speaking. Severe dysphagia[26] following cervical spine fusion using rhBMP products has also been reported in the literature."

I was stunned to my core to read this. And to think it was issued only seven months after my surgery, and only a month or so after I consulted Dr. Virella about my dysphagia. It certainly seemed to explain the effects I experienced then, and will always experience, in my throat and neck. However, as with so many aspects of my accident and recovery, it was another silver-lining case of: It could have been so much worse. I was fortunate compared to others whose necks had been treated with BMP.

Because the Notification stated that such side effects had been reported in the literature, I was surprised that Dr. Virella was unaware of this topic. The first paragraph in the Notification states that BMP was not even approved for use in cervical spinal surgeries! (The Notification stated that it was approved only in the lumbar spine, which is in the tailbone area where over-stimulated bone growth would not have any nearby critical tissues to impact as it would in the neck.) Even if Dr. Virella was not aware of these potential complications ahead of time, I thought it would have been helpful for him to have notified me once the Notification was issued. In fact, the Notification states this: "Patients treated with rhBMP in the cervical spine should know the signs and symptoms of airway complications, including difficulty breathing or swallowing, or swelling of the neck, tongue, mouth, throat and shoulders or upper chest area, (and) that they need to seek medical attention immediately at the first sign of an airway complication."

Given that I had moved to Ohio when I learned about this, and since I had never gotten worse, I did not try to contact Dr. Virella. I had survived without the more serious complications suffered by others, and therefore my only thought was that I was thankful. I continue to experience the effects of a constricted throat, such as occasional

---

26 Dysphagia means swallowing difficulties.

swallowing difficulties, restricted singing range, and neck cramping, but I still regard myself "a lucky stiff."

Chapter 21 – Crossing the U.S. in 32 days

At my retirement party on August 31, 2006, about a year before my neck accident, they displayed a U.S. map showing my planned ride across the country the following April. It was no secret that in retirement, I was planning to ride my bike even more than I already had been.

Crossing the country by bike had been a background dream ever since Bob Brown talked about his 1976 BikeCentennial trip when I first hired him in 1979. In 2005, a Nestle colleague's husband, Paul Butler, whom I had known for 20 years, was going to ride from Los Angeles to Boston in May and June to fulfill one of his long-held dreams. It got me thinking more concretely about my doing such a ride when I retired in two more years. When Paul and I did weekend rides, we'd talk all about the details of his upcoming tour, and I truly was excited for him. I wished I were going too!

The day before his departure, I called Paul to give him best wishes and said I'd be talking with Celeste (his wife who worked in my division at Nestlé) for updates along the way. When I called her on the evening of his departure to see how the send-off and first day went, I had to leave a message. Little did I know that Celeste was not home because she was with Paul in the hospital. It's almost beyond belief, but misfortune struck only 11 miles after they got started. The rider in front of Paul hit a bump and fell, which caused him to fall as well, and he broke his collarbone. His dream tour ended after only 45 minutes.

After Paul recovered physically and emotionally, we began talking about his trying the cross-country ride again. I said that if he waited until 2007, I would be retired and could do it with him. He agreed, and a plan was hatched. We decided to use a different tour company,

America By Bicycle, since he'd heard they were better. The route was better too, from Astoria, Oregon to Portsmouth, New Hampshire. During my rides in 2006, I fantasized about my future all-day jaunts across our country. Leading up to my actual retirement, however, my e-mails with Paul were not answered. Three weeks after retirement I competed in the Malibu Triathlon in which I was riding the bike leg on a Nestlé relay team (the same team and event as in 2007 which is described on page 4 and page 61). I saw Paul and Celeste there, and he broke the news that he had decided not to ride across the country after all. It was perfectly understandable, as Celeste had had a very serious medical problem that potentially was life-threatening, and this changed Paul's life priorities. He didn't want to be gone from Celeste for eight weeks.

Because the bike tour was going to impact niece Megan's wedding and the annual Mercurio houseboat trip, I decided to change to a different cross-country route offered by America By Bicycle. It was called the Fast America Ride, lasting only 32 days, and it was in the spring, not the summer. It had several advantages: far less cost, cooler weather, and I'd be home for the Tour de France and the other summer events. Of course, it was a lot tougher with an average of 115 miles per day instead of about 80, only one rest day instead of five, and the route from Los Angeles to Boston would not be quite as scenic (I didn't think). However, the challenge of 115 miles/day with only one day of rest intrigued me. I had done three-day rides at that rate, and I was in better shape than then. I'd have seven months of retirement to get in even better shape. But mostly, it would be a harsh test and therefore more rewarding.

Right away my mileage and efforts increased. I took 60- to 100-mile training rides at least four days a week, sprinkled with interval training up hills. People would ask how I was enjoying retirement and what I was doing, and about all I could say was that I was cycling[27]. Every pedal stroke had me imagining myself on rural tree-lined roads

---

27 I also started a small consulting business to assist companies with their labeling and regulatory affairs, but it was secondary to my bike rides.

cruising across the country. I felt like Walter Mitty, always dreaming of a glorious biking scenario.

It didn't take long, however, for doubts to cloud my head. Was I training hard enough? Was I resting/recovering enough? Would I get ill or injured from over-training and ruin the big tour? I had read four different training books in addition to *Cycling After 50*, but all they seemed to do was confuse me more on the ride-hard-versus-recovery question. And, my Nestlé cycling friend, George, got me thinking when he said he wouldn't necessarily want to do 115-mile-average days because what fun would it be to be wasted every night?

Therefore, I leaned toward getting a coach to help prepare me. I researched on the Internet and found a group from Greenville, SC who looked good and whose cost was reasonable. I spoke to the head coach, and her approach seemed like it would work well. It was $150/month, and we'd communicate primarily using their online program of receiving weekly training prescriptions and my reporting results. The coaching would be based on my reported heart rate data using a heart-rate monitor. I would begin in December and continue for the four months leading up to the big ride.

It was the best $600 I could have spent. I hadn't realized what a relief it would be leading up to the April 23 departure date not to have to worry whether I was training properly. Removing that worry made those training months a joy, even if some of the workouts were killers. They assigned me to Coach Jim Cunningham[28], and when I'd whine about how hard some of his assigned rides were, he'd say "Pay now or pay later." Jim was a great coach and became a good friend. He answered every question I could come up with. I know that without him, I would have ridden many more hours and miles because he had me take more easy recovery rides and more days off than I would have on my own. His techniques worked too, if I do say so myself. I did the Solvang Century 36 minutes faster than my previous best, and even pulled away from my ex-

---

28 While I was under Jim's tutelage, he broke away to form his own coaching service, Greenville Cycling & Multi-Sport. http://www.greenvillecyclingcenter.com

racer friend Dave Preszler in the hilly second half. Three weeks later I did the Solvang Double Century two hours faster than my goal, and 3½ hours faster than the Davis Double Century I'd ridden in 2005. That ride proved to me, with only three weeks to go before the Ride Across America, that I was ready and would enjoy my tour, and not be wasted every night.

As you'd expect, my anticipation increased as April 23 neared. I don't think I thought about anything else. I had over-deliberated every last aspect of what I'd need to take, what I'd wear, how many PowerBars and PowerGels I'd need (knowing that they also provided foods at the rest stops), what to buy for rainy days, which tires would be light enough yet provide sufficient flat protection, which maps to take along, and which chain lube to use. According to their rules, the weight of my suitcase could not exceed 35 pounds, and the backpack for the SAG van could not exceed 15 pounds. This had to include my computer not only to write a blog for interested "fans", but to maintain my consulting business. In the final two days, I was weighing my bags using my bathroom scale and shedding excess items that were "good to have" but not essential.

Finally, Sunday, April 22 arrived, and we drove to Costa Mesa in the late morning to check in. I met other riders, the staff checked my bike and helmet, and I completed all their paperwork. Brother Rick made a point of stopping by to wish me good luck. We had a two-hour orientation meeting with the four staff, and learned the rules and who my 24 new riding buddies were. We had a Brit, a German, a Dutchman, three Canadians, two 65-yr-olds, and some ex-racers. Two were women. By the time our tour ended, I can say they were all close friends, fabulous bicyclists, and great people in general. I was lucky to be in such an extraordinary group.

I couldn't get to sleep in my anticipation, and it seemed like I was awake all night. But that didn't slow my energy and excitement the next morning. We all headed west (the wrong direction for our eventual goal!) about two miles to the beach to perform the wheel-dipping tradition: If you ride across the country, you dip your rear wheel in the departing ocean, and your front wheel in the arriving ocean. After a full group photo at the beach, we headed east to begin our trek.

Rather than relating here the entire, wonderful, 32 days on the road, I will refer the reader to the blog I updated each night, filled with dozens of photos! The site is www.BikingCrossTheCountry.blogspot.com.

I can say that writing a daily account and uploading photos were an added "burden" to each day's scurrying about. I had two roommates in motel rooms with two beds and a roll-away bed for the third person (we took turns). The room also had to accommodate our three bikes, our bags, our helmets and other cycling gear. So, finding a place to type on the computer was a challenge, especially since one of my roommates (Kasper, the Dutchman) also was blogging each night. But finding the *time* was the real challenge; we had to eat, clean and lube our bikes, shower, eat, meet to review the next-day's route sheets, eat, wash clothes, make phone calls to family, eat, and sleep. Our wake-up calls were at 5:30 in order to eat, load our bags, and get going in time to ride another 95 to 150 miles. When I needed to use the computer, sometimes my roommates would already be asleep so I'd type in the bathroom or the motel lobby. But of course, I'm glad I made the effort to do the blog because not only will I always treasure the memories I would have forgotten, but so many family and friends wanted to share my daily experiences across the country.

Suffice to say, the trip and all its aspects were truly a highlight of my life. Except for a couple days, our weather was perfect[29]. The routes were scenic, the staff super, the new friends wonderful, the riding fun, and the cycling challenging. I was in such good condition that I had the energy to explore off the set route occasionally, such as riding 12 extra miles in Arizona to tour the Meteor Crater. I tried to stop at historical markers, knowing I could catch up (or not fall helplessly behind). I developed a "reputation" for my many visitors and for stopping to visit Nestle

---

29 If you look up my blog, check out days 12 and 13 if you want to see some scary weather stories.

facilities along the way[30]. Although riding in draft lines helped, I didn't require them; I could venture off alone and still make good time. Every day was thrilling. I never was ill, and I had only one minor mechanical problem and only two flat tires.

On the final day, we rode together into Salisbury Beach, just south of the New Hampshire border, wearing our America By Bicycle jerseys. With the crowd cheering, I had chills running down my body and tears running down my cheeks. We had been so focused on our busy daily routines, following our route maps, biking, and eating, that we hadn't had enough time to reflect on the feat we were accomplishing. But riding up to the beach, it hit all of us. Some thought quietly to themselves, while others whooped it up out in the surf. We all posed for the front-wheel-dipping photos, plus a final group shot.

After about an hour of celebration and photos, it was time to shut down. My bike went to a local bike shop to pack and ship home. A friend who used to live in L.A. was there to celebrate with me. That night we had our final banquet, with speeches from each rider and staff member, and many memories shared. I have stayed in contact with almost all of them. After my broken-neck accident, Annette sent an e-mail to one of my closest new mates, Dave Thompson, informing him what happened. He forwarded it to the whole group, and I soon received get-well cards and e-mails from nearly all these new friends.

---

30 I had seven visits from friends or family, and I stopped at three Nestlé factories or research labs. One visit was with son Brian in Marysville, OH who drove the 45 minutes from Ohio State. Another was from sister-in-law Cathy the angel, who drove 8 hours to surprise me.

Chapter 22 – A new bike, presumably with a better fork

Being able to drive again in April, 4½ months after my accident, meant I started doing a lot more chores. I would get the dry cleaning, pick up some groceries when we needed something special, and occasionally get take-out food so Annette wouldn't always have to cook after her long work days.

However, the big event in May was Katie's wedding. In March we had flown to Seattle for her shower, and now we would head back. We didn't have anything to do except attend, since Katie had arranged everything already. I did write a formal toast to give, but that was about it for any preparation on my part. The weather in Seattle and out at the Salish Lodge was perfect on wedding day, May 24, and I fulfilled the promise I made to Katie exactly six months earlier while lying in Emergency; I walked her down the aisle. What an emotional moment that was.

As with so many other happy moments we had experienced in the past six months, this one also had its tragic counterpart. Two days before we flew to Seattle, our dog Lily died. This one was entirely my fault, was preventable, and I felt terrible. I had seen rats in our back yard, so I put out rat poison in a place where I was *certain* this little dog couldn't get it, but I was wrong. She became listless on the Monday before the wedding, and we took her to the emergency vet clinic where they gave her blood, platelets, oxygen, everything they could think of, but it was too late. Annette especially was devastated; her second dog gone in three months. Annette mustered up everything she had to still attend the wedding and make the best of it. We wondered what else could go wrong during the year that started with the previous summer's houseboat trip. We kept thinking each bad event would be our last. It didn't work out that way...

My next appointment with Dr. Virella was in late May. I could drive to this one myself! He confirmed I would be continuing PT for several more months, and that August 1 was still the anticipated date I could start cycling outdoors again. He even gave me encouragement regarding riding, and suggested I get the bike he rode, a Specialized Roubaix.

In my PT, I told the therapist about my sore back and neck muscles and wondered if he could try something new. That very morning he had me lie on my stomach instead of my back, and he actually massaged and did pressure-point therapy. What a difference! I even exclaimed aloud, "Where have you been all these months?" which got a chuckle from everyone in the room. After his massage, I enjoyed increased range of motion and less tension. It's true that it didn't last, but it sure felt better and I assumed (maybe incorrectly) that it would make me heal faster. From that day on, I used a metal rod device to press on the trigger points on my back, and it really did make me feel a lot better.

Three weeks later (June 23) was my next Dr. Virella appointment, but this time there was momentous news! The PT had done a formal evaluation of me the day before and gave me a written report to give to Virella. I was able to read for myself that he was recommending I discontinue PT. He said I'd maxed out on the weight program and my range of motion, and that the tightness would dissipate only with time, not with additional PT or exercise. It surprised me, but Dr. Virella agreed!! Only three weeks earlier he had confirmed I would be doing PT until October, and now he was saying I was done with it. Also, he said I didn't need to wait until August 1 to ride the bike, but could start on July 7 when we returned from Sarah's wedding in Minneapolis.

July 7? Wow, that would give me three additional weeks of bike riding before the Blue Ridge Parkway tour. That was 60% more time to train! This was huge! Buried in my excitement were Dr. Virella's compliments that I had recovered well for someone with my injury, and that he didn't need to see me for another year! Annette had me promise to ask pointed questions about whether I should even attempt to ride the Blue Ridge Parkway tour given its difficulty and the intense training it would require to prepare for it. The doctor was on my side! He said I should simply play it smart and watch out for numbness in my extremities, which would indicate I was overdoing it.

I was overjoyed with this news, although I still had a nagging caution in the back of my mind with regard to riding a bike on the street again; I wasn't sure that I would be able to bend my neck upward enough, nor withstand the soreness I always had while maintaining my neck at the extreme of its upward bend. Outwardly I just assumed it would work.

I got to celebrate my assumed return to the streets with others in the San Fernando Valley Bike Club a week later at a dinner party for the club. While there I got to meet Stan Motzkin for the first time, who had assisted me when I had my accident. Even though I had spoken to him on the phone after I got home from the hospital, he had some additional memories from that day to share with me, and it was strange to picture myself once again lying on the street like that, blessed to be still alive.

Since we were going to Minneapolis soon, I had to hurry to buy my new bike, which is always a treat for an avid cyclist. I had read about the advantages of getting a custom bike, fitted to one's exact measurements and riding styles, and people who had them swore by them. But custom bikes are very expensive. As a compromise, I located a custom builder about an hour away who agreed to help me find the stock bike closest to being a custom for me. Before I went to see him, I made a spreadsheet of 10 top name-brand stock bikes with their various tube angles and lengths and so on (such data can be found on each bike's website). In each case, I chose the manufacturer's "comfort" bike in their lineup, since I already knew I needed a bike with the handlebars raised slightly and other frame angles that afforded more comfort for endurance riding. After the bike maker did all his measurements and we discussed the kind of riding I would be doing, he located a bike from my chart that looked spot on: The

Specialized Roubaix, the very bike Dr. Virella suggested I get (but only because he owned one). It turned out that the other bike shop in Simi Valley (not my regular shop) had the exact Roubaix I wanted – the "Expert" version. Specialized had about six levels of the Roubaix, each with increasingly expensive components and lightness of the frame. The Expert was the third-best level, and weighed only about 17.5 pounds. I bought the bike the day before we left for Sarah's wedding, and while I was gone they would raise my handlebars even higher using a special stem I had used during the ride across the country[31].

Off we went to Minneapolis on July 2 for a wonderful wedding and family reunion, yet probably 70% of my thoughts were on getting to (try to) ride a bike again as soon as we returned home. My stationary riding in the hotel fitness room in Minneapolis would finally end this boring form of training, and I could soon become a real bicyclist again (I hoped!).

---

31 I had used this stem to make my all-day rides for 32 days more comfortable. By raising the handlebars a couple inches, you don't have to bend over so far and it eases your neck and back. When I finished the cross-country ride, I reinstalled the original stem and set aside the new one, not thinking I'd ever need it again. Who knew I'd need it again so soon?

Chapter 23 – In the saddle again, but the losses mount

What a huge blast we had in Minneapolis! The wedding was wonderful, and the reception was one of the best I'd ever been to. However, the next day, Janet let us know that Mom had been hospitalized the day before with a choking and breathing problem. We didn't know too many details yet, but it did not sound good. We wouldn't be able to see her for at least a couple days.

It seemed that every time there was something wonderful and exciting in our lives, it was accompanied by something very bad:

- Megan's wedding and then Dad's heart attack
- Getting a new car, and the next day The Cabin burned down
- A nice Thanksgiving, and then my bike accident
- My getting to shed my braces, and then Becky dying
- My getting to drive again, and then the car crash
- Katie getting married and Lily dying in the same week
- Sarah getting married and me getting to ride again, and Mom entering the ICU -- from which she didn't recover.

Life can take unexpected turns, and you just have to take things as they come, do your best, and trust in God that everything will somehow be okay. But what a string of linked events like this! Of course, we all hoped this trend would end. Leaving Minneapolis, we could only hope that the news about Mom would get better.

As soon as we arrived home on Monday, July 7, I went to the bike shop. I put my new steed into the trunk, zoomed home, and Annette and I decided to go for a short ride immediately. I was dying to see if I could actually cycle again. As you know, as optimistic and goal-oriented as I'd been since my accident, I still never knew whether my neck would allow me to ride when the opportunity finally arrived. I donned cycling clothes for the first time in 7½ months, getting a little weepy realizing what a major step this was in my recovery. We took pictures of me getting on the new bike, and then I was ready. I kept looking both ways from the driveway before setting out, to *ensure* no cars were anywhere in sight.

Finally we took off! What was going through my mind? I figured I'd be hooting and hollering with joy, but what I was focused on were using the mirror and straining my neck up enough to see in front of me. Annette rode behind, and I kept trying to see her in the mirror and get used to its field of vision. The pedaling and mechanics of riding felt fine since I was actually in pretty good shape, and if I'd actually think about it, I was thrilled to finally be on the road again. But my conscious enthusiasm was held in check because I kept testing the mirror, and straining my neck upward to make sure I wasn't riding crooked or into a parked car.

At the end of the short 2-mile ride, I basked in the glory of being alive, leading a normal life again, and now riding a bike again. *I'd done it!* Even holding the handlebars at the uppermost location, I could not lift my neck quite enough to see forward constantly, but I was determined to make it work. Now, I would focus on the symbol of *full* recovery, the Blue Ridge Parkway.

The next day I started my new routine – actually my old, pre-accident routine – of riding in the cool of the mornings. I decided to ride in the new housing tracts to the north of us where there were few cars and wide bike lanes. Now I truly did feel like my old self (other than the tight and sore neck muscles, of course), climbing the hills and working hard, and feeling the fresh breeze in my face.

However, I quickly had to adopt a new riding style that continues to this day and may be necessary always –

taking special measures to soften my ride over bumps. The first thing I did, even before I left on my first ride, was to make sure the tires were inflated to no more than 100 psi (I used to inflate them to 125 psi). Less pressure means a softer ride. While riding, I had to pay extra-close attention to any irregularities in the road surface (bumps, holes, or rough surface) so I could either avoid them or absorb any shocks through my legs by standing slightly on the pedals. If I didn't cushion myself like that, such that the jolt went through my butt on the saddle, it would transfer directly into my neck, which *hurt*!

I also found that I needed to drop my neck the moment I was going over a bump, because the jolt would cause more intense pain if my neck was bending upward to its limit. In order to see far enough in front of me to anticipate these bumps and irregularities, I needed to brake constantly going down hills to slow my speed. Of course, I already was a little slower down hills (and on the level, especially into a wind) because of the high handlebars and the fact that I must grip the very tops of them in a decidedly upright body position. I was clearly the opposite of aerodynamic (which makes me appear NOT to be a fast, serious cyclist). I went up hills well, but slowly down them, abetted by my braking to save my neck!

In all my years of cycling, one of my greatest joys, which was now going to be forever hindered, was sight-seeing. I had always loved taking in all the scenery wherever I rode. However, from now on, my line of sight was pretty much straight in front of me. Only if I deliberately hold the handlebar with one hand and twist my torso to the side, can I take in the sights to my left or right (and I can do that only when everything around me and on the road is perfectly safe and predictable).

I also found myself doing something psychological, so to speak: Every so often, particularly after going over a bad bump, I'd look down to check my forks. I knew by then that carbon-fiber forks would not show any indication of impending failure, but I would look nonetheless to satisfy my paranoia. And if ever I was going fast down a hill and I noticed my speedometer approaching 28 mph, it would trigger a "wow" reaction that I could have been going so fast when I flipped onto my head and still survived.

I managed 14 miles that first day. I knew I needed to ride as often as I could, every day if possible, to prepare for the Blue Ridge Parkway ride in just 9 weeks. However, the very next morning was already a rest day from the bike, as I flew to Sacramento, met Rick, and we went to see Mom at her hospital in Woodland (Janet was stuck in Minneapolis). Mom was still in the ICU, and did not look good. If we asked her how she felt, she'd answer "fine," but if there was no talking for a few moments, she would utter "oh please, oh please." She couldn't eat because she didn't have an adequate swallowing reflex. As I recall, Rick and I mostly tried to keep her calm by talking with her or singing songs; she occasionally would try to hum along with us. It was another emotional time for the Mercurio family, to know that Mom was declining toward her end.

When Janet arrived the next day, I came on back home since Mom's condition didn't seem to be changing. I rode 25 miles in the afternoon, back and forth through the housing tract to the north of us, afraid to venture out farther where the main traffic was. My neck was sore, especially by the end, and it felt good to finish and lie down. Lying flat was, and still is, the only time I can not tell anything is different about my neck; it feels completely normal.

The next day I did decide to venture out on a longer ride. This time I attached a rack to the seat post and carried my towel roll. I figured if my neck or back was getting sore or stiff, I could stop every so often, lie back with the roll under my shoulder blades, and stretch. Well, it did and I did. It must have looked pretty wild to see a helmeted guy in a colorful jersey lying on his back on the sidewalk with his arms stretched behind his head. Carrying a towel roll looked funny too, as another rider caught up to me and asked if I was headed to the beach.

I dared my way out to Los Angeles Avenue, figuring it was time to conquer my demon of riding past where my accident had been. The fellow who joked about me riding to the beach was still riding with me as we approached the spot, and I told him what was going on with me and how it would be my first time riding there again. It was momentous to me, but he didn't seem to share my gravity and kept talking about something else, and before I knew it we were past the spot and it was done. So much for a solemn milestone!

The ride that day was 33 miles, so I'd gone from 2 miles to 33 miles in just four rides (over five days). My neck was always tight and sore, but I was motivated to keep pushing along. I had stopped to lie down and stretch my neck/back twice, about every 12 miles. The next day I rode 25 miles, including to the top of Santa Susana Pass. My hill-climbing ability was feeling pretty darned good, plus I could give my neck frequent rests on the hills because, considering my slow speed, I didn't need to always be watching very far ahead. I could let my head drop, and that always relieved the pain for a few moments.

By then, the daily reports from Janet indicated that while Mom had some good moments, she was not improving overall. In fact, some doctors were giving pessimistic prognoses. After talking with Rick and Beth, we decided to fly back up to Winters. I left on Sunday, as soon as I finished a guest lecture (food labeling) at USC. Mom was mostly sleeping, but did not look good and still could not eat. The next two days were terrible, as she was declining noticeably and we had to make the decision to remove her IV and let her die. The hospital suggested she go under hospice care back at her residence in Davis. On Tuesday, July 15, an ambulance moved her back and they put her into her own bed. Just as the nurses finished getting her all tucked in and parted the curtains for us to see her, she stopped breathing. We quietly sang *Silent Night* to her as we watched her neck pulse gradually come to an end. Our wonderful, saintly, most-perfect mom was gone. At least gone from our physical earth, but we all knew where she was now.

Since she had been suffering, the end was actually a blessing and somewhat of a relief. The finality is still so difficult, however, so there was lots of crying to go around. After several phone calls, all four of us went to a restaurant to reminisce and plan ahead. The service would not be for about five weeks to allow time for Rick and Beth's scheduled trip to join Megan and Manuel in Venezuela, and for Sarah and Anthony to return home from their honeymoon in Argentina. The next day I went home. Janet said she would be okay taking care of things. Cody was down in Los Angeles attending a summer course in musical theater, so she was suddenly without day-to-day responsibility for others, with time to tackle necessary arrangements in a more orderly fashion. I arrived home midday, tired, but decided I'd better get back on the bike. I squeezed in 14 miles on that hot afternoon, my thoughts lost sadly in what incredible parents I had and what exceptional lives they gave us.

Chapter 24 – Pedaling, Pushing, Punishing

The next morning I drove to Calabasas to join several members of the San Fernando Valley Bike Club for what they said was going to be an easy 32 miles. It actually *was* easy, and Mark, who had come to see me in the hospital, was impressed with how well I was doing on only my seventh ride; he said I was pushing the pace faster than he wanted to go since this was a recovery ride for him. That made me realize I was progressing pretty well, and stood a good chance to accomplish the Blue Ridge Parkway ride if everything continued to go okay. And I was still two weeks ahead of when I originally was going to get to start riding a bike again, so I felt like this was all gravy in my plan to complete my goal.

I was so inspired by my progress that I rode 49 miles the next day, and 56 miles of the hilly Santa Monica Mountains the next. My average speed was starting to creep up as well, from the 14s and 15s, to by now the mid 16s mph. I continued to stop every 30 minutes or so to lie on my towel roll on someone's side walk. I always slept as soon as I was done with a ride, as my regimen was quite difficult, making me very tired, and my neck and back would be sore. But I wanted to push through the difficulties to achieve the big ride in September. By August 1, my original date to get to ride again, I had pedaled 716 "bonus" miles, and done two rides of 70 miles or more.

One of those 70-mile rides was with Bert on July 31, our first together in about six years. We met in Santa Paula, about 25 miles from Simi, and checked out each other's bikes, looked at my X-rays, and generally caught up on a few things. Then the ride began on quiet streets with virtually no one around. And I promptly fell. WHAT?? Within a half mile, we had come to our first stop light. As we stopped, I was looking up to tell Bert about the historic building across the street and did not notice that my front wheel came to rest on a thin piece of plastic. Well, flat plastic has no traction, and when I clipped out of my pedal and put my right foot down on the street, the front wheel just started sliding to the left, and I couldn't stop it and I fell sideways right down onto the street.

Luckily there were no cars around, and Bert and the few people who witnessed it called out to make sure I was okay. I was. I immediately got up and was laughing and also trying to understand what had happened (that's when I saw the piece of plastic). The first thing I said was, "Don't tell Annette," because I feared my cycling comeback would end as suddenly as it had begun if she heard that I had fallen in the middle of a street.

We went ahead with our ride, and had an impressive average speed that day of 17.4 mph. I felt like my cycling ability was back! I was even climbing the hills faster than Bert, and he had always been faster than I had.

If I could just keep up this pace, I figured I would successfully complete the Blue Ridge Parkway ride. I began to fantasize about crossing the "finish line," and would get emotional each time this thought ran through my mind. If only I could finish the ride, I would have conquered my injury that could have, should have, paralyzed or killed me. These sobering thoughts were ever-present.

Over the next five weeks I really pushed myself. I was riding HARD. I increased my intensity and mileage and long hill climbs, but I needed more recovery than before my accident. I absolutely had to rest a long time after a hard ride, and needed more days off than I used to require. On another ride with Bert we did 90 miles at over 17 mph, but I needed two recovery days. Would I be able to ride five days straight on the Blue Ridge Parkway?

I also began my massage therapy. I had been thinking massage would help my neck and back, but I hadn't really searched for a real therapeutic massage therapist. One day in early August, I was on an errand in a strip mall and I saw a store sign for what I was looking for. So, I dropped in and made an appointment. My first session was heaven/hell, mostly the latter. Diana, who I teasingly called Dr. Torture or the Wicked Witch[32], was good at finding sore spots and then working on them to extend my pain over much of the 90-minute sessions. But she promised it was helping me! To tell the truth, I enjoyed these massages and felt better as time went on. Also, to save money (haha) I bought the special package of 12 hours, allowing me frequent torture sessions in the weeks leading up to the big tour. Diana and I got to be pretty good friends since there's lots of time to chat, except when you're howling that it hurts.

On August 26, just 13 days before the tour was to begin, I set out to ride 100 hilly miles through the Santa Monica Mountains. It was hot and windy, which didn't help, but I was getting through it okay until I had about 20 miles to go, at which point I was suffering and wanted to stop. Still, I had to get home, and kept plugging away. The final few miles were agony; all I could think about was getting off the bike and lying down. When I finally rolled in, my odometer read 99.4 miles; later, Bob Brown kidded me about not riding at least 0.1 mile more so I could round it up to 100 miles, but I was so beat that day, I could not have ridden 0.001 mile more. Even though I had accomplished 99 miles and about 6000 feet of climbing, it actually discouraged me about whether I could ride five straight days at about that same average distance with an average daily climbing of 9000 feet.

All I could do was keep pushing ahead. However, I also needed to recover to be ready for September 8. I had six rest days over the final two weeks, something I never could have afforded had Dr. Virella not given me the extra three weeks of riding. Who knows how wiped out I might have been had I needed to ride hard every day right up to September 8?

Three of those six rest days were for the weekend of Mom's memorial service. Janet had arranged everything and planned out a wonderful program. On Friday, we joined my siblings and Aunt Sharilyn (Dad's sister) to set up the niche at the cemetery and spread ashes at the Hawthorne house (the new owner let us) and at the high school track where Dad ran, and the tennis courts where

---

32 Obviously a joke if you saw how attractive she is.

Mom played. That night the whole family went to a restaurant to celebrate Sarah's and Brian's birthdays, which were the next day and the previous day, respectively. Then we had Mom's touching service and a reception in the morning, and an afternoon gathering at a restaurant where Mom and Dad had eaten several times per week for 20 years. How sad when your parents are gone, and what a tumultuous year for our family! We hoped the bad streak had ended. I looked with optimism to the future as several friends/family asked about my upcoming bike tour and congratulated me on my recovery.

On August 27, a Wednesday, I phoned the bike shipping-box company to make sure everything was set to FedEx the bike the following Monday to Charlottesville. We were flying to Washington, D.C. on Saturday, September 6, and driving south to Bob Riggs' home that evening[33]. I needed the bike to be at Bob's house so I could assemble it the following morning prior to joining the tour group that afternoon in nearby Waynesboro. Well, it's a darned good thing I happened to call that Wednesday just to check on things! The fellow said I needed to mail it THE NEXT DAY, not the following Monday. Even though the literature with the shipping box I had ordered had said to allow five days for shipping, the fellow said that meant five workdays, and the next Monday was Labor Day. Plus, he said I should allow an extra day just in case – meaning I needed to ship the next day. Luckily, John Bruton was staying with us for a couple weeks while waiting for his new apartment in Pasadena to become available. He and I got out the instructions for assembling the box and packing the bike, and spent the next couple hours getting it done. Additional luck in having John staying with us was that he had his truck, which could carry such a big box; he drove it and me to the FedEx office the next day, and off it went to Bob's in Charlottesville.

For my final five rides I took over the next week, I used my Bianchi bike. Interestingly, its handlebars, while

---

33 Bob and his wife Dot had been Annette's close friends since she first moved there in 1980, and they became my friends as well. We always stayed at their house when we visited Charlottesville. Dot passed away in December, 2006.

adjusted upward as high as they could go, were still not as high as what I was used to with the new Specialized Roubaix bike. I tested it to see whether I'd be able to raise my neck enough to ride it, and it seemed like it would be okay. Sure enough, I was able to ride as long as ever (including a 73-mile very hilly ride) and my neck was fine (as much as it ever was, relatively speaking).

In all, I felt ready for the Blue Ridge Parkway tour. My riding had progressed to where I was almost as strong as before the accident. The picture in my mind of finishing the ride came more frequently, and I continued to get emotional and sob for a few seconds every time it happened. I was confident, yet there were still doubts about whether I'd be able to ride at this challenging level for five straight days. Deep down, I knew I would give it everything I had, to fulfill this symbolic quest I'd been focused on for 9½ months.

Chapter 25 – Our own bike path

There I was, crying in the peloton. We had just gotten started after taking our requisite photos with everyone's camera in front of the huge Blue Ridge Parkway sign, and I caught myself saying, out loud but quietly, "I actually made it here." It was one of those times you didn't know you were speaking aloud until your ears heard you saying it. Regardless, it started the tears.

We had arrived the day before in Washington, D.C. as scheduled, rented our car, and driven to Charlottesville. We were lucky that the hurricane Gustav had just finished passing over as it headed north. For the previous several days, I was wondering if our ride would be hit by Gustav, but we got lucky. The next morning I reassembled my bike and test-rode it for about 5 miles around Bob Riggs' neighborhood.

The ride started in Waynesboro, Virginia, which is only 30 minutes west of Charlottesville. We drove there Sunday evening to meet the others, who had all met in Asheville, North Carolina, where we'd stay when the ride ended. They were then shuttled in the tour van up to the starting point. I would be doing the opposite and would have to get "shuttled" (with Annette) back to Charlottesville at the end.

When their van arrived I met Paul Wood, his brother, Curtis, who would assist Paul, and the other 12 riders. Out there in the parking lot, I showed my X-rays to Bob and my roommate for the tour, Nick. Of course they were duly impressed with all that metal in my neck.

We had a wonderful and diverse group of riders -- two women and 11 men. The oldest was 67. Doug and Jo, the youngsters in the group, were from London. Two were from mid-Illinois, Nick was from a Chicago suburb, a food-company CEO was from Montana and North Carolina (he split his time between the two), and one was from Colorado. Over the next two days, word got around about my accident and my fused neck, and everyone expressed their best wishes and congratulations on my having recovered enough for this ride.

We learned that evening over dinner that the standard procedure the next morning was to load all the bikes on the van again and drive the few miles up to the start of the Parkway. An option, although Paul said that no one had ever done it before, was to ride to the start. Bob and I decided to do that.

The next morning was beautiful with a clear blue sky and warm temperatures. PERFECT. Bob and I got ready early and left at the suggested time so that we'd meet the van when it arrived at the Parkway. Bob predicted we'd get there way too early, and he was right. It was 7.75 miles, uphill only near the end, but not too difficult. We arrived at the big sign that said "Blue Ridge Parkway" and took our own photos of each other, and read the historical marker explaining when and how they built the Parkway. It was a WPA project in the 30s, but was never fully completed until the 1980s. It was meant only as a pleasure drive, so it is never a throughway for travelers going from one city to another, and there is not a single stop sign, traffic light, or services for the entire 469-mile length. The speed limit is 45 mph all the way. There are mileage markers posted for every mile the entire distance, and we were going in the ascending direction, Mile 0 to Mile 469.

Bob and I finally sat down and just talked for an hour or so until the van arrived. It actually was nice to get fully caught up on work[34] and family. Once everyone was there, we took all the photos and it was time to begin.

Immediately the Parkway was incredible! Beautiful scenery in all directions, and we had the road to ourselves except for an occasional motorcycle or two. It took me only a few yards to realize how wonderful it was to be there, and I uttered those words to myself, cried for several seconds, and then settled in to absorb all the good feelings. It felt like the best ride I'd ever been on.

---

34 Bob had been giving me several consulting projects over the previous 9 months. I was once his boss, but now he was my boss.

The hills naturally spread us riders out as the morning went on. Bob, Bert and I rode mostly together, but not always. The Parkway has many view-point turnouts, and many of us took advantage, especially I since I couldn't see the sights left or right very easily while riding. We were high up, so the views on either side were of the valleys to the east or west. at Mile 58 next to a river, we had our lunch, which was a nice spread of sandwich makings, cookies, sodas, energy drinks, and all sorts of welcomed goodies.

I must say, Paul and Curtis were fabulous hosts. They catered to our every need, and waited on us hand and foot: "May I grab you another drink? Let me get you a chair. Which drinks and other foods shall we buy for you?" They put up bike racks and canopies (when needed) at the stops.

After lunch we proceeded to the lowest point on the entire Parkway, at the James River. There was a visitor center for the once-active locks and dam there, and I spoke to the ranger about the history of the river boats in the old photos on the wall.

Then came our 13-mile, 3300-foot climb. I felt good, and just kept plugging away at my own comfortable pace. It turned out that I was pulling away from the others. I arrived alone at the final rest stop, Mile 77, took a nice break, and then decided my tired/sore back and neck would feel better lying down, so I headed off on the final nine downhill miles. When I rode into the Peaks of Otter Lodge at Mile 86, a National Park Service hotel, Paul had just arrived and was unloading the suitcases. I found my room key, took my bag, and got to shower, lie down, nap, and enjoy the memories of the perfect first day.

I eventually awoke and shared stories of the day with some of the others. I enjoyed a short walk to view the attractive scenery and lake. I slept well that night. As I fell asleep, I remember thinking that I was probably going to be able to complete the ride. I didn't want to make any premature conclusions, but I felt strong and my neck felt okay. A smile was on my face.

The next day we were given a staggered departure schedule, based on our riding times from the day before, so that we would arrive at the lunch stop at approximately the same time. It rained pretty hard for the first 60 miles. Luckily I had good wet-weather gear, so I was okay. The only bad part was that the clouds obscured our views of the valleys, and sometime even waterfalls near the roadway; you could hear the waterfall but not see it. Riding on the Parkway was still incredible though. It was like our own bike path, over hill and dale, with little farms and chalets occasionally. I wished I lived in the area to be able to ride it all the time.

As we pedaled along, we established a "pattern," as one fellow put it. I would pass most of the group up the hills, and they would pass me down the hills. Again, the entire route was fantastic. What a beautiful bike ride!

Waiting for me at the motel that evening (Mile 174) were Dave Thompson (from the ride across America), his wife Sandy, and their dog Abby. They were pulling their boat from their Canadian residence to their Florida home, and since they were passing through that part of Virginia, Dave had decided about a month earlier, while visiting in Simi Valley, to ride with us for one day. They were right there as I rode up, and what a pleasant rendezvous!

The motel owners had two Labrador Retrievers who looked just like Abby, and one was even named Abby. While everyone was cleaning and re-greasing their bikes because of the rain, the dogs were providing entertainment because they wanted us to throw them big sticks to chase. Even if we threw them into the little lake, they'd plunge in after them. I could not throw those big sticks very far; it was another of my "stiff neck" handicaps.

The next morning, Dave and I were the last to leave. It was fun getting to ride together again 16 months after we pedaled into Salisbury Beach, Massachusetts. This third day was the longest of the tour, 125 miles, and rain was again predicted. If I could finish this day with no problems, I surely would be able to complete my epic recovery ride.

Right away we passed one of the tourist highlights of the Parkway, Mabry Mill. I remembered being there in 1978 when my first wife and I were on a three-week driving trip across the country and back; we got a photo then, and it was crowded then, but on this day but it was too overcast to want to stop and no tourists were in sight.

After our first rest stop it began raining, and it didn't stop for the remainder of the day. It didn't just rain, it poured! We were completely drenched -- rain jackets can do only so much. Those who saw me use my towel roll to stretch my back[35] laughed because I was lying on a picnic bench facing upward with the rain just pelting me. But what did it matter since I was already soaked?

The rain was coming down too hard to have our lunch from the van, so Paul told everyone to go ahead and sit down at a restaurant (Mile 241) and just order off the menu. He was nice like that! When we entered, we had to shed as many of our wet clothes as we could and make do, still wet. We all ordered coffee or hot chocolate to warm up, and that was sure a comfort.

Even though no one was too anxious to venture back out in the pouring rain, eight of us eventually did, and headed off for the remaining wet 52 miles. I learned later that six of the group decided to ride in the van the rest of the way, being as they were the intelligent ones.

The dicey part of our remaining miles involved a detour. We were in a group of five when we had to exit the Parkway and ride around a construction area where they were repairing the road. Unfortunately, there was a quarter-mile section of dirt road, and our bikes, gears, chains, and clothes all got covered with mud. Once the muddy section ended, I had to stop and wash off the chain and cassette using my water bottle. I was able to get most of the mud off, but the chain still made gritty noises for the rest of the ride.

Nick eventually caught up to us, and we six rolled into the small village of Blowing Rock (Mile 293) just before dark. It had been nearly nine hours of riding time, and 11 hours total to complete the ride that day! An epic day for our epic tour.

The van didn't arrive until over an hour later since it was helping to light the way for the two Londoners who

---

35 Since we had a support van, I put my towel roll in it and used it at most of the rest stops, even though I had discontinued carrying it on my bike's rack a month earlier.

finished in the dark. During that hour, we had to stay in our wet clothes trying to warm up in our rooms. What a relief when we finally got to shower and get into warm clothes! During dinner, we reflected on the day: It was less scenic due to riding through clouds, and we had over 10,000 feet of climbing, but if you had to ride in rain, the Parkway was the best place to do it. After cleaning my bike with a hose at about 10 pm and then lubing the chain, I finally got to go to bed. I was smiling all over.

Rain was still coming down as we departed the next morning for our 95-mile day, but it was intermittent and eventually dried out in the afternoon. So, we had some scenic clearings again, as we climbed over 10,000 feet that day too. It was an option to climb up Mt. Mitchell[36] and back down again, and Bob, Bert and I decided against it since it would be too cloudy for any views. Thus, we were the first ones to arrive in Asheville that afternoon. We departed the Parkway at Mile 377 to wind down into the town, and noticed many other cyclists out riding and training since we were near a big city. Besides, it was clear weather late in the day, so it was perfect cycling.

Surprise surprise as we rolled up to the door of the elegant Haywood Hotel in the center of downtown – there was Annette. She had just arrived, having decided to drive all the way to Asheville instead of stopping partway and then driving to the Parkway's end the next day, which was her original plan. So, Nick lucked out to get our room to himself, since I needed to rent a room for Annette and me. The dinner that night was at a lively tapas restaurant where each table of four ordered small ala carte dishes to share. We all had huge appetites by that fourth night, so the waiters had to keep taking and delivering orders constantly from our big group. As I went to bed that night, I finally knew for sure that I would complete my goal.

---

36 At 6684 feet, the highest peak in the eastern United States.

Chapter 26 – Standing ovation

Over and over during the ride, and more frequently as the week went on, I would picture myself finishing and it would set off an emotional surge in me. On the final day, I was spilling over in that department, although I tried not to let on.

We all left the hotel as a group and stayed together as we wound our way through Asheville's streets and roads leading back to the Parkway. Because we had left the Parkway northwest of Asheville the day before and re-entered to the south at Mile 390, we actually missed 13 miles of it. Therefore, technically I cannot claim to have ridden the entire length of the Parkway, but I'm going to anyway! We rode more miles through Asheville than if we'd stayed on the Parkway.

Once we got onto the Parkway, it was a long gradual downhill to the French Broad River. As was usual on descents, I fell behind everyone else. Once we crossed the river, however, there was a 35-mile climb that was almost constantly uphill until we reached the highest point of the tour (6047 feet). In the first mile of the ascent, I passed the large group and Paul yelled out "Contador" as I went by (Alberto Contador was a good climber who won the Tour de France in 2007). I looked farther up the hill, and figured I'd try to catch and ride with whomever it was way up ahead in the distance.

As I gradually got closer, I couldn't decide who it was. It took me a long time to finally catch the person, and it was Jo. I'd never seen her climb like this before, and she was barely winded. It turned out that she was a good climber but had wanted to ride with Doug, so she never "showed her stuff." She said that on this final day, they decided to let her ride her own pace, and they'd meet at the 46-mile rest stop and then go together from there. Well, I soon learned who the best climber was on this tour (although Paul and Bob may have been too, but they preferred to usually ride with others).

Jo and I went at a pretty fast pace the entire climb. I found myself pushing harder than I had the entire week because I was in front and she was back there chatting away, not sounding tired at all. I didn't want to slow her down! Finally I was so pooped that I announced I was going to have to slow the pace, and she said she was relieved because she couldn't maintain my pace either. But still, we were cruising, and I learned that she was a competitive rower, and how cycling is a good conditioning sport for rowers. We had some beautiful views along the way because the clouds were intermittent, and a highlight was a cascading waterfall across a valley that made me wonder how many other spectacular sights we missed during the week because of the weather.

Finally we reached the scenic turnout at the top of that eternal climb. It was our rest stop (Mile 431) and Curtis was waiting there alone in the mist. Jo and I ate and rested, and then she decided to go *back down the hill* to meet Doug and ride up again with him. Can you believe that? Instead of staying there alone, I pressed on and figured I'd spend my extra time at the lunch stop instead of in the cold mist.

Twenty miles later, after a 10-mile descent followed by a 10-mile climb, I arrived at the lunch stop. The view was incredible! Two of the cyclists were already there since they had ridden in the van part of the way. As the three of us were enjoying the food and the views, who should drive up but Annette. It was funny that she was there not because she wanted to have lunch with us, but because she'd made a wrong turn. She meant to drive to the end to meet us, but she accidentally turned up the road into a visitor center parking lot where we happened to be.

Eventually everyone was together at the stop, eating leisurely, taking photos, making phone calls (yes, a spot with cell phone service), and comparing stories from the 4½ days behind us. I even called FedEx to arrange my bike pick-up on Monday from the hotel back in Asheville. Since the remaining 18 miles to the finish were almost all downhill, I knew for sure I'd accomplish my goal. Again, I was getting emotional, and Paul even gave me an early congratulations.

The only thing that could prevent me from finishing was a crash, so I was thinking how I'd need to be extra careful, especially since there would be about a dozen tunnels where a light is required. During those final two days, we had 25 tunnels. Some were short, so we didn't really need our lights, but others were pretty long. We needed to use a light not only to guide us through, but so that any oncoming cars would see us. I carried my light in my "bento box" holder on my top tube, and would pull it out, turn it on, hold it in my left hand, and shine it where needed. At the other end, I would turn it off and put it away. This required a lot of "messing around," so I went especially slowly.

It finally was time to depart the lunch stop for the final segment of the tour. I had chills, and it wasn't from any cold weather! Bob, Bert and I left together, but since those final miles were all downhill, and since I was going even slower than usual, everyone else passed me and got to the finish before I did. I didn't care. I was teary most of the way, as the emotions bubbled over for all the miracles of the past 9½ months and the blessings in my entire life. I wasn't really even supposed to be here according to the doctors, yet I was, and able to complete a physically epic ride.

I watched each mile marker as it passed behind, and when I got to 468, my sobbing started. I was getting shivers during that final mile by myself, my mind filled with thoughts of gratitude and accomplishment. Then I could see everyone up ahead standing in groups on a bridge. Suddenly the tears came full force, and I was openly bawling as I rolled in. I passed some of the guys who were yelling or cheering for me, but I couldn't acknowledge them in my state. I saw Bob, Bert, Annette and a few others on the far side of the bridge. I pulled up and stopped, and I think when they all saw how much I was crying, they left Annette and me alone for the first several minutes. I just could not stop openly crying. I think everyone was fully realizing the significance that finishing this ride meant to me.

Eventually I gained some control and we all congratulated each other for finishing the ride. There were lots of hugs, handshakes, and photos in all possible permutations among us. Many told me I was an inspiration to them.

The Park Service sure picked a scenic, but desolate, spot to end the Parkway. It was on the bridge over a beautiful river that has a humdinger name: Oconaluftee. Interestingly, except for a few posters at the Mile 469 marker giving an overview, there is nothing there acknowledging the beginning or end of such a treasure that the Blue Ridge Parkway truly is. No visitor center, no tourist stands, no bathrooms. Not even a city nearby. In one sense, we were in the middle of nowhere.

Paul and Curtis had to load all the bikes on top of the van except mine, which fit in our rental-car trunk. There was no room in our back seat for Bob or Bert because it was folded down to hold the bike shipping box. We followed the packed van and trailer all the way back to Asheville. It was a long drive, and a lot of the way I was still lost in my thoughts. I called and left a few "accomplishment" messages with Katie, Brian, and Rick.

We eventually arrived back to the Haywood Hotel and set a time for dinner. We had our own room at the restaurant for this final celebratory evening. Paul spoke about our accomplishments, and we toasted our success. Doug and Jo had graciously bought champagne, and we had more toasts. Paul told some funny stories and memorable twists from our five days.

Paul then began to give out special T-shirts to some riders for a unique accomplishment or trait, some funny, some serious. After giving away about seven or eight of the T-shirt awards, he pulled out what he said was his final one. He began to say something about this cyclist having done something beyond what he could adequately describe, and then he stopped and his hand covered his eyes. He paused a few moments, too emotional to continue. At that point he just walked down the table and handed me the T-shirt. Then something happened which was a highlight of my life and I will never forget: *A standing ovation.* One by one, everyone stood up to recognize my recovery and triumph.

I was shedding tears once again. I could barely look up. I waved in thanks, but I didn't know what else to do. When they sat back down, I managed a meek "thank you," but I was gushing in gratitude for their kindness and support. I wished later I could have said something appropriately expressing my feelings and thanks, but I just sobbed and smiled.

During the evening, it struck me that virtually all the riders, at one time or another, talked about how I was an inspiration to them. It also continued to impact me just how fortunate I was for my second chance. Something was stirring inside me that there must be something more to my good fortune than simple luck.

That night, I was thinking how my goal to inspire others had come true. I'd said I wanted to inspire others with my recovery, and indeed, it seemed like my successful bike ride and full recovery had helped in at least a small way to show that one can make life what you wish it to be with the hand you're dealt, and that there are always silver linings.

As time has passed since that ride ended, I also look back with fresh eyes on the miracle of my survival, the marvel of my successful surgery, the wonder of my recovery, the outpouring of love from family and friends, and what life means. Although I was never a spiritual person, I found myself drawn to a belief that there actually must be a loving God who has a hand in people's everyday lives. He is with us and supporting us as well as He can, given what we do independently, and surely that love will be a source of inspiration for me as I move on in my life.

Epilogue

The glow of finishing the Blue Ridge ride continued with me for some time, especially since I then wrote about it for the final two chapters of this book. I finished the book on the exact day of the one-year anniversary of my accident, although I have revised it in small ways for many additional years prior to its being accepted for publication.

I noted back on page 132 that the various good things happening to us or to me were usually, unfortunately, accompanied by something bad. We kept hoping that string would end, and so I was particularly cautious when I completed the Blue Ridge ride and was reveling in my accomplishment. Would something terrible happen to balance my joy? I'm happy to report NO, there was nothing, unless you want to count the sudden economic collapse in the world.

So, following my ride and book manuscript, I was a bit empty. I continued to put in lots of cycling miles and to ride in centuries, but on a broader scale: What now?

For so many months I always had this book as my "project," but when I put the pen down, I wanted to focus on a future goal. Lucky for me, I had one.

It was something I'd dreamed about for 25 years, and seriously for 10 years: A year-long trip of the Great Loop Cruise. This is a boating adventure -- another epic -- that covers 7000 miles of waterways around the eastern half of the U.S. and Canada. Ever since I started reading detailed books about it in 1999, I planned to begin the trip in spring, 2008. At my Nestle retirement party, they posted a map of the route and everyone shared in my exciting plan for the near future (after the bike ride across the country).

Not only did my bike accident push the date back, but even had I not had the accident, it had to be postponed because I never found anyone who wanted to go with me, despite seven years of talking it up with numerous "candidates." (Annette had never wanted to do it.) My search for companions kept coming up empty: 1) friends weren't available because of work; 2) even if retired, they now had grandchildren or parents to care for; or 3) one year was far too long to be gone. I had about 2000 people who wished to join me for a week or two during the summer of the trip, but none wanted to be my permanent mate.

With the date pushed back by at least two years because of the accident, suddenly some candidates surfaced who would be retired by 2010. Bruce Perry, my high school friend, would join me for the first three months and final five months, and brother Rick would be first mate for the middle five months. In late 2009 I would purchase a used "yacht" approximately 34 to 40 feet in length in the Chesapeake Bay area. I would begin to provision it and learn how to operate it on a couple of trips before winter, and then drive back for final provisioning and practicing in Spring, and plan to depart in May of 2010.

Sure enough, I bought a 40-ft boat in August of 2009, and gave it a perfect bicycling name -- Breaking Away[37]. The following March, I drove across the country and took both my bikes so my mates and I could explore around the stops along the way. It all went according to plan until Bruce and I reached Canada in late June, when he decided to "jump ship" because he didn't enjoy the adventure as much as he thought he would and also needed to attend to business back home. Therefore, I canvassed the landscape to piece together visits from family and friends to fill in, albeit with time gaps, the months that Bruce had planned to accompany me. In the end, it all worked out. It's a gross understatement to say it was an incredible and highly adventurous grand tour, concluding in late June, 2011.

---

37 "Breaking Away" is the term given to a single or group of cyclists in a race who pull away from the rest of the group. It also happens to be the title of every avid cyclist's favorite 1979 movie.

The route is easiest to describe with a map[38]:

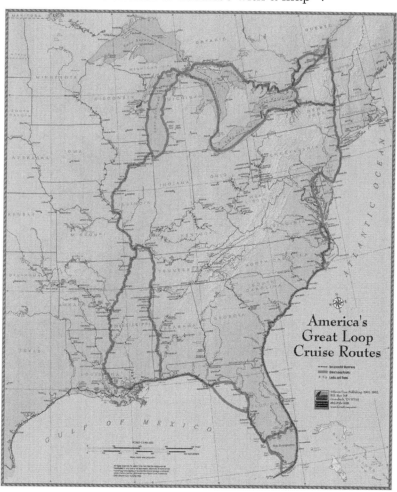

We headed up the Chesapeake Bay to the Delaware River, down to the Atlantic, north into NY Harbor, and up the Hudson River to the Erie Canal in Albany. I traversed the canal to Lake Ontario, crossed the lake to Canada's Trent-Severn Canal that weaves through Ontario into Georgian Bay of Lake Huron, and then cruised west to Lake Michigan after a short side trip to Lake Superior. My brother and I followed the west side of Lake Michigan to

---

38 From: America's Great Loop Cruisers' Association, Summerville, SC

Chicago, sailed right through its downtown, and hooked up with the Illinois River, which flows to the Mighty Mississippi. From there, just 200 miles downriver, we headed up the Ohio River for a short distance to a giant lock that lifted us into the Kentucky Lake/Tennessee River system. Many scenic miles later, a canal took us south to the Tombigbee River that leads to Mobile, AL on the Gulf Coast. From there, I sailed to Key West and finally up the Intracoastal Waterway back to Virginia and Maryland. If the reader would like to read more about my Great Loop adventure, my blog is still online at www.BreakingAwayOnTheLoop.blogspot.com.

I've continued to ride long distances once the boat trip ended, highlighted by a 3120-mile ride from Butte, Montana to Anchorage and Fairbanks and about halfway back in 2012. This trip was with four others, including Bob Brown and Bert Stock. If the reader is interested in this adventure, my blog is www.BikeToAlaska.blogspot.com.

I wonder what's next in my life? Whatever it is, or not, I've had a blessed, wonderful life. I'm thankful to God that there have even been opportunities for a "what's next?" for me, following that high-speed rendezvous with the pavement in November, 2007. I plan to treasure every day I'm here on earth. See you then!

Postscript: February, 2010

The court trial began on September 15, 2009. The defense, primarily the fork manufacturer, enlisted an expert engineer witness, who also was an accomplished racing cyclist. He argued that evidence indicated a foreign object, like a stick, must have been thrown into my spokes. He theorized that it then lodged up against the forks and broke the nine spokes before finally breaking the forks. Since the five cycling witnesses at the accident site looked for but didn't find any such object, he argued that it must have been thrown into the bushes hidden from view.

The jury did not agree, siding with our two expert witnesses instead. Using microscopic and electron microscopic analysis of the broken fork, the experts concluded that the blades spontaneously snapped, and that it was the broken fork that sheared off the nine spokes. The evidence also showed air pockets and a too-thin design in critical stress areas of the fork, suggesting poor manufacturing and design flaws.

The jury rendered its verdict on September 24. In early November, the judge heard arguments brought by the defense on a point of law regarding the medical-insurance payments, which potentially would have reduced the jury's award. Prior to giving his decision, the defense offered, and I accepted, a compromise between what they were seeking and what the jury had awarded. The long ordeal of my accident finally ended on February 2, 2010. All that's left is a stiff neck, soreness, and occasional pain. And many blessings for which I will be eternally thankful.

Made in the USA
San Bernardino, CA
16 November 2014